W9-BLE-963

HOW MANY TIMES
CERTAIN WORDS
APPEAR IN THIS BOOK

Cool—22
Really—69
Nice—28
Awkward—6
Embarrassing—3
Coffee—23
Sublime—1
Weird—6
Bittersweet—5
Death—1
Random—15
Love—78

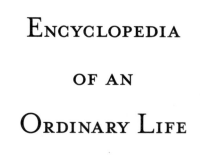

Encyclopedia

of an

Ordinary Life

ENCYCLOPEDIA
OF AN
ORDINARY LIFE

BY

AMY KROUSE ROSENTHAL

[VOLUME ONE]

CROWN PUBLISHERS   NEW YORK

Published by Crown Publishers, New York, New York.
Member of the Crown Publishing Group, a division of Random House, Inc.
www.crownpublishing.com

CROWN is a trademark and the Crown colophon is a registered trademark of
Random House, Inc.

Printed in the United States of America

Not responsible for lost or stolen property.
Not responsible for the weather, the moon, or scalding nature of soup.
Not responsible for the extra *s* some people add to the word *occasion.*
Not responsible for the short, edible window between
the banana is not ripe enough and the banana is rotten.

See page 223 for permissions credits.

DESIGN BY ELIZABETH VAN ITALLIE

Library of Congress Cataloging-in-Publication Data
Rosenthal, Amy Krouse.
Encyclopedia of an ordinary life : volume one / Amy Krouse Rosenthal.—Ist ed.
I. Rosenthal, Amy Krouse. 2. Women—United States—Biography. I. Title.
CT275.R7855A3   2004
973.931'02'07—dc22   2004011332

ISBN 1-4000-8045-2

Not responsible for the lovely ladybug
or purple iris
or flirtatious glance
that was yours to enjoy
but which you did not notice.

2 4 6 8 10 9 7 5 3 I

First Edition

Encyclopedia of an Ordinary Life was written in Chicago at
Julius Meinl Coffeehouse and Katerina's Café.

Reader's Agreement

You agree not to reproduce, replicate, or reprint any of the material in this book without our consent. When reading this book, you agree to give it your undivided attention—that means no pretend half-reading while calling and placing an order for Thai takeout. At the end of each page, you agree to thrust your arms upward and emit a loud, staccato *Hey!* just like circus performers do at the end of each stunt. You agree that, on any given weekend, there are way too many mattress sales. You agree that while black is technically the absence of color, it makes more sense for it to be all the colors combined, and, likewise, that white should be the peaceful, blank absence of color. As for nonfiction and fiction, you agree those should be switched as well; nonfiction should be the non-true one, and fiction, true. You obviously also agree that *playwright* should be spelled *playwrite*. You agree that, yes, it is astounding, the human ability to eat at seemingly inappropriate times, like after a funeral, or at a charity luncheon featuring a Holocaust survivor flown in from Amsterdam. You agree to refrain from complaining on Monday about it being Monday, and acknowledging on Thursday that it is almost Friday. You agree to see for yourself just how perfectly this book cues up with Pink Floyd's *Dark Side of the Moon* and *The Wizard of Oz*. You agree—because it is just so sad and ridiculous—to refrain from talking on your cell phone while working out at your health club or walking your child into school. You agree to provide us with your Visa number (please include expiration date) and approval to spend up to five hundred dollars on merchandise from the current Anthropologie catalog. You secretly admit that, yeah, your favorite word is your own name—don't worry, that's normal; studies have shown that there is an actual physiological response upon hearing your name, that hearing your name releases some sort of *happy hormone*. This makes sense: Remember when you were a kid and they did roll call? Didn't you feel good when they got to your name? "Ava?" "Here!" And even now, when you pass someone in the hall at work, don't you feel a certain tingle when the colleague says, "Hi, Ava," instead of just "Hi"? You agree that, yes, we all suffer, perhaps even daily and deeply, but who wants to hear it? You agree that some women look sophisticated wearing a shawl, others foolish.

Yes, I agree to these terms.

Name_____ Date _____

Visa # _____ Expiration Date _____

Foreword

I was not abused, abandoned, or locked up as a child. My parents were not alcoholics, nor were they ever divorced or dead. We did not live in poverty, or in misery, or in an exotic country. I am not a misunderstood genius, a former child celebrity, or the child of a celebrity. I am not a drug addict, sex addict, food addict, or recovered anything. If I indeed had a past life, I have no recollection of who I was.

I have not survived against all odds.
I have not lived to tell.
I have not witnessed the extraordinary.

This is my story.

—AMY KROUSE ROSENTHAL, age 39
Chicago
June 2004

Characters

JASON . . . . husband

JUSTIN . . . . older son

MILES . . . . younger son

PARIS . . . . daughter

CHARISE . . . . close friend and collaborator

The action all takes place in America
at the end of the twentieth century,
beginning of the twenty-first.

Contents

Acknowledgments

I would like to thank you for reading this book.

Publisher's Note
We invite you to add your name
to the list of people who have
ever read this book and who were
personally thanked (by e-mail) by
the author. Click on *Thank You* at
encyclopediaofanordinarylife.com.

ORIENTATION ALMANAC

N

The following is an attempt to provide the reader, particularly those of you who come to this in a distant and certainly different era, with plain facts about American life at the beginning of the twenty-first century, the backdrop against which this book was written.

World Population
    6.16 billion

Top CNN Stories 2000–2005
    September 11
    Dot-com bubble burst
    Enron scandal
    Iraq War
    Clinton and Lewinsky
    Harry Potter
    Atkins/Low-Carb Diet
    Gay Marriage

Countries in Power
    United States
    China
    Russia
    England
    Germany
    Japan

To Whom Americans Attribute Power
    Movie stars
    Rock stars
    Sports stars ——————————————
    Rich people
    Major political figures

Cost of Living Averages
    Stamp . . . . 37¢
    Pack of gum $1.00
    Quart of milk $1.80
    Gallon of gas $1.90
    Loaf of bread $2.50
    Pack of cigarettes $3.80
    Movie tickets $9.25

Hardcover book $24.95
Pair of Levi's $32.00

Confirmed Planets

Mercury
Venus
Earth
Mars
Jupiter
Saturn
Uranus
Neptune
Pluto

Highest-Rated Television Shows

Super Bowl
World Series
NBA Championship
Academy Awards
The Sopranos
American Idol
Reality-television shows

What We Call the Other Driver When Angry

Bitch
Asshole
Fucking bitch
Fucking asshole

Ways We Exercise

Jogging
Biking
Spin classes
Treadmill
Lifting weights
Pilates
Yoga

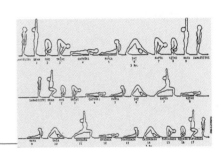

Common Signs

Employees Must Wash Hands Before Returning to Work
Not Responsible for Lost or Stolen Property
Please Do Not Throw Sanitary Napkins, Tampons, or
Paper Towels in Toilet
No Parking
Pedestrian Crossing
Beware of Dog
No Soliciting

Machines We Own

Television
Computer
Cell phone
CD player and iPod
Washing machine and dryer
Dishwasher
Coffeemaker
VCR and DVD player
Video camera
Digital camera
Microwave oven

Popular Kids' Names

Jacob	Emily
Michael	Hannah
Matthew	Madison
Joshua	Ashley
Christopher	Sarah
Nicholas	Alexis
Andrew	Samantha
Joseph	Jessica
Daniel	Taylor
Tyler	Elizabeth

Childhood Rhymes

Eenie Meenie Miney Moe
Catch a tiger by the toe
If he hollers let him go
Eenie Meenie Miney Moe

I went to a Chinese restaurant
To buy a loaf of bread,
He asked me what my name was
And this is what I said:
Elvis Presley
Girls are sexy
In the bath
Drinking Pepsi
Had a baby
Named her Daisy
Had another one
He was crazy
So this is what I said:
Supersonic idiotic overloaded disconnected bubble butt.

We must
We must
We must increase our bust
The bigger the better
The tighter the sweater
The boys depend on us

Most Popular After-School Activities

Seasonal sports (soccer, football, basketball, baseball)
Karate, Tae Kwon Do
Chess
Dance (ballet, jazz, hip-hop)
Gymnastics
Music lessons (piano, violin, guitar, drums)

Colors of the Rainbow
  Red
  Orange
  Yellow
  Green
  Blue
  Indigo
  Violet

Colors of the J. Crew Catalog
  Orchid
  Grape
  Pacific
  Grass
  Ink
  Cantaloupe
  Oasis
  Lilac

Sex ———————————————————
  Kissing
  Breasts fondling
  Manual stimulation
  Oral sex
  Penetration

Excuses
  Kid sick
  Working late
  Baby-sitter canceled
  Car wouldn't start/in shop
  Stuck in traffic
  Something came up

How We Answer the Question "How Are You?"
Good
Fine
Stressed out
Tired
Great
Busy ─────────────────

What We Take to Feel Better
Advil
Cigarette (tobacco, marijuana)
Glass of wine
A beer
A cocktail ──────────────────
Valium
Prozac

What We Say When We Bang Our Knee on the Corner of the Table, Burn a Hand on a Hot Skillet, or Get Frustrated Trying to Untangle a Computer Cord
Shit!
Fuck!
Fucking shit!
Goddamn it!
Jesus H. Christ!

Numbers and Codes We All Memorize
Phone number and home address
Cell number
Pager number
Fax number
Pin number (cash machine card)
Social Security number
E-mail password
Amazon returning customer password

Home security system code
ID number for voice mail

Acronyms That Are Common But Confusing

NASDAQ (tech stock index)
NASCAR (association for race-car drivers)
ASCAP (society for authors, composers, and publishers)
NAACP (African-American organization)
NAPSTER (online music entity)
NASA (space program)
NETSCAPE (computer browser)
NESCAFÉ (coffee company)

Dialogue as We Pass Coworker in Hall

Hi. How're you?
Good, thanks, you?

Hey. What's up?
Not much. You?

Letters in Our Alphabet

A a B b C c D d E e F f G g

H h I i J j K k L l M m N n O o P p

Q q R r S s T t U u V v W w X x Y y Z z

Common Slang

Dude
What up
Yo
Whack
Sweet
Bling-bling
My bad

Most Frequently Used Words

Hi

Bye

Okay

No

Yes

EVOLUTION OF
THIS MOMENT

965
Sei Shonagon born.

▼

1965
One thousand years later AKR born, Chicago, Illinois.

▼

1965
Agatha Christie writes the epilogue in her autobiography:

Long walks are off, and alas, bathing in the sea; fillet steaks and apples and raw blackberries (teeth difficulties) and reading fine print. But there is a great deal left. Operas and concerts, and reading, and the enormous pleasure of dropping into bed and going to sleep, and dreams of every variety. . . . Almost best of all, sitting in the sun—gently drowsy . . . And there you are again—remembering. "I remember, I remember, the house where I was born. . . ."

▼

1966
AKR's first word:

more.

▼

1969
From this point on, draws constantly.

▼

1975

Notices and likes certain signs and phrases.

For example: Billboard for new subdivision going up in her town
says GREATEST EARTH ON SHOW. Clicks for her.

They've reversed the circus saying, greatest show on earth . . . cool.

And loves this sign at friend's pool:

THIS IS OUR OOL.
NOTICE THERE IS NO P IN IT.

1976, Card to parents

TO a pretty couple

THats been maried for
a dozen years
so hears a
dozen eggs

LOVE
AMY
Beth
Joe
Kate
ELLEN

Twenty-some years later, gets inordinate pleasure out of creating
anniversary card for her parents, Paul and Ann:

HAPPY (PAUL AND) ANNIVERSARY

1976

Discovers Ziggy.
Remains an obsession throughout teen years.

▼

1977

Paints little Lucite box with words *Pop's Corn,* fills it with a bit of popcorn, and gives it to Dad on Father's Day. Father appropriately responds by keeping it on his bureau for the next twenty-five years.

▼

1978–1990

Links new vocabulary words with the person she first heard use them:

Father: Integrity
Jeff: Nefarious
Peter: Industrious

▼

1982

English teacher, Mrs. Lowey, instructs class to keep a journal.

▼

Summer 1984

Gets job at popcorn shop painting decorative tins as gifts.
Boss tells her she is good at coming up with timely, sellable ideas (like painting the phrase *Girls Just Want to Have Fun* and the *Ghostbusters* logo)
but that her work is messy, poorly painted.
She agrees, but doesn't like the executing, just the idea part of it.

▼

1985

Tries to write fiction in creative writing class in college.
Keeps writing the truth, stuff that actually happened. Teacher says
make things up. Ultimately, alters her assignments and is
supportive.

▼

1986

Journal from year in Paris:

*I think 90 percent of what/who we are is never really
verbally communicated. . . .*
*I like to write things down—moments, memories, lists, quotes, thoughts.
Compulsively sometimes.*
*I need to gather all the thoughts that are locked in my head and put them on
paper. Will my memory ever fail me? Maybe that's the precaution I'm taking.*

▼

1986

During summer internship at ad agency, boss
gives pivotal three-word critique of her research-related writing:

Express vs. Impress.

▼

July 9, 1987

From journal:

Mom thinks I'll be a writer someday.

▼

1987

Worries about mastering the segue.
Is there a kind of writing where each paragraph does not drift
fluidly and seamlessly into the next?

▼

July 20, 1987

Tells manager at Baker's Square that
restaurant's sign shouldn't be round.

▼

1988–1997

Lands job as advertising copywriter.
Loves distillation of ideas, concise writing,
short attention span compatibility.
Job pretty much a blast.

———

Upon meeting for first time, boss Jeff tells her,
You don't look like a writer.

———

Sees that the word *Levi's* is in the word *television* . . .
Tries unsuccessfully to sell campaign around the tagline
Levi's have always been a part of television with clips of famous
TV characters wearing Levi's.

———

Thinks her client Kraft should do something called
The Krafterschool Special, à la the special after-school movies that
aired in the seventies.
Goes nowhere.

▼

1989

Reads *The Day I Became an Autodidact,* by Kendall Hailey.
Writes author and receives letter back. Thus begins Pavlovian
habit of writing earnest letters to authors whose work has
moved her, a fact that embarrasses her later when she comes
to think of it.

———

Drawn to charts, signage, unusual formats for writing.
Produces items for her own amusement.
Discovers word-oriented artists Barbara Kruger, Jenny Holzer,
and later Stephanie Brooks.

▼

1992

Cocreates *Oyster,* a very short-lived, very experimental,
very ego-driven zine/newspaper.

▼

1993

Introduced to artist Charise Mericle Harper.
Meet every Thursday afternoon from this point on to occasionally
collaborate on work, provide mutual sounding board, and
much-needed, rose-colored encouragement.

▼

1993

Takes playwriting workshop with Neo-Futurists theater company
founder Greg Allen, whose philosophy resonates with her:

Work must reflect the randomness of life, with its incessant, merciless, almost humorous bombardment of highly contrasting emotions and experiences.

▼

1995

Discovers writer David Shields in *Harper's Magazine*. Crazy about his work. Soon thereafter reads his book *Remote.* Writes him. They correspond for a time.

▼

1995

Discovers Paul Auster, whose book *The Red Notebook* reinforces the beauty and validity of coincidences/serendipity. Writes Auster. Cherishes his simple reply on elegant stationery.

▼

1996

Records material in ad agency studio with engineer Stump Mahoney.
Sends it off to Ira Glass at *This American Life.* Receives call one gray Sunday afternoon. Work not right for their show, but he gives her crucial feedback: Work is way too random and scattered. Think about organizing material by subject in some way.

▼

1996–1997

Writes for *Might* magazine. Is given joyous free rein to write choppy, random, handwritten, segue-free column.

Later develops similar column with solely parent-focused
material for *Parenting* magazine. Good gig but abruptly ends after a
few months when the magazine staff changes in their move
from San Francisco to New York.

▼

1997
Might folds. When she tries to sell her uncategorizable work to
local newspaper, editor tells her,

Well, Amy, I'm afraid you're a Might *writer in a* Might*less world.*

———

After nearly two years of rejections and dead ends,
gets first piece in *Utne Reader* magazine.

▼

1997
Almost writes/codirects short piece for MTV,
but after initial green light, buzz, and excitement, and telling
everyone about it, whole thing falls apart.

▼

1997
Begins contributing commentaries and listlike pieces
to Chicago's NPR affiliate, WBEZ.
Station receives unusual feedback from listeners,
along the lines of

Hey, I can do that. I for sure can do that. I'd like to do that. Can I do that?

———

Around this time, reads quote:

You don't have to necessarily be the best at what you do—there's always someone better. Instead, be the only one who does what you do.

1997
Decides to leave advertising.
After a year, she finally gets an agent. He sends out manuscript for *The Book of Eleven*. Receives wide range of well-crafted rejections.

1998
Publishes *The Book of Eleven.*
Well received by press and readers. Assumes book will be best-
seller, thinks that is just how it works.
Sales are educationally underwhelming.

1998
Finds new home for choppy, random column: *Chicago Tribune*
online magazine. Upon securing this gig, signs up for
Internet access.
Writes this column weekly for next four years, though midway
through it moves to amused.com.

1999
Discovers *The Pillow Book of Sei Shonagon.*
From Introduction:

The Pillow Book *is the precursor of a typically Japanese genre known as*
zuihitsu *("occasional writings, random notes"). . . . The structural confusion
of* The Pillow Book *is generally regarded as its main stylistic weakness;
yet surely part of its charm lies precisely in its rather bizarre, haphazard
arrangement in which a list of "awkward things," for example, is followed by
an account of the Emperor's return from a shrine . . . and then a short,
lyrical description of the dew on a clear autumn morning.*

This is tremendously exciting to her. Enlightening. Reassuring.

1999

Has art show of sorts at local coffeehouse/gallery.
Work is conceptually okay, but poorly executed.

> EMPLOYEES MUST
> HOLD HANDS BEFORE
> RETURNING TO WORK.

▼

1999

Tries to put together a couple of photo-essay concept books.
One idea: Photograph and document the contents of various
people's refrigerators (celebrities and ordinary people alike).
Another: women's purses.

———

Reads Alain de Botton's book *How Proust Can Change Your Life*.
Becomes fixated on Proust-themed books and biographies.
A few years later, upon reading third book by Alain de Botton,
sends e-mail to him.

▼

2000

Reads James Thurber for first time.
Particularly drawn to his autobiographical "casuals" for
The New Yorker.

▼

2000

Publishes second book, about motherhood.
Incorporates charts and an index.

▼

2000–2002

Creates *Writers' Block Party Audio Magazine.*
The critical success/commercial failure theme continues.

▼

2001

Begins compiling all the pieces from weekly columns.
There are no thematic headings;
For organizational purposes, decides to aphabetize material
according to first letter of each piece. Soon sees that this could
make for an interesting format for a book.
Wonders if she shouldn't just save all this material for a novel
down the road, when she finally *gets serious* and tackles fiction.
People often seem to imply this kind of nonfiction writing
she does is only a means to an end,
a breezy warm-up for inevitable fictional oeuvre.

▼

2001

Publishes third book, again about motherhood.
Contains longer pieces—essays—a writing form she likes but that
she finds reminiscent of school writing assignments.

▼

2001
Discovers writer Leonard Koren, author of *13 Books*
and *Wabi-Sabi*.
Sends e-mail. Kind reply. His wife's name is Ziggie.

▼

Spring 2002
Tells Charise about idea of writing not an autobiography exactly,
but rather a biography of one's self, interviewing people in
your life as if writing third-person biography.
Charise thinks it sounds cool, and continues to ask about it,
though Amy does not do anything with it for a while.

▼

Late summer vacation reading 2002
Several books seem to come together, making a statement;
things begin to gel.

———

*Spend it all, shoot it, play it, lose it, all right away, every time. Do not hoard
what seems good . . . for another book. . . . The impulse to save something
good for a better place later is the signal to spend it now.*
—Annie Dillard, *The Writing Life*

———

*What stops me from taking myself seriously, even though I'm essentially a
serious person, is that I find myself extremely ridiculous—not in the sense of
the small-scale ridiculousness of slapstick comedy, but rather in the sense
of a ridiculousness that seems intrinsic to human life and that manifests itself
in the simplest actions and most ordinary gestures.*
For example, I can never shave without starting to laugh; it seems so idiotic.
—Flaubert to Louise Colet, as retold in *The Art of Travel*
by Alain de Botton

"Do you think I can be a writer?"
"I don't know. Do you like sentences?"

—Conversation between teacher and student, as retold in
The Writing Life by Annie Dillard

To simultaneously strive and let go . . . don't be concerned with the
fruits of your labor.

—*The Heart of Yoga* by T. K. V. Desikachar

Hone your craft, have fun, don't go for "art."

—Douglas Adams, *The Salmon of Doubt*

▼

Fall 2002

Knows it is time to put a book together, though can't yet see what
it is, what it could be. Her material feels scattered; lacks anchor,
structure, and purpose. Sets biography of self/interview idea in
motion by contacting several key friends, sending off list of
questions via e-mail. Soon realizes this would not work as a book
but might be interesting incorporated *into* a book.

Further reading helps crystallize:

I called [Bob Dylan]. . . . I said, "I am totally wigged out and I don't know
what I'm supposed to be doing, and I've got a lot of pressure to incorporate
what's going on." He said, "Go back to your roots. Take out the albums that
you loved and play those songs. Get your band together and rehearse those
songs, and then you will start writing." And that's what I did.

—Sheryl Crow, *Rolling Stone*, October 31, 2002

But writing with simplicity requires courage, for there is a danger that one will be overlooked, dismissed as simpleminded by those with a tenacious belief that impossible prose is a hallmark of intelligence.

—Alain de Botton, *The Consolations of Philosophy*

———

Many things that I would not care to tell any individual man I tell to the public, and for knowledge of my most secret thoughts, I refer my most loyal friends to a bookseller's stall.

—Montaigne, as quoted in *The Consolations of Philosophy* by Alain de Botton

———

Montaigne offered so much information on exactly how commonplace and private his own life had been—why he wanted to tell us:

That he didn't like apples:
"I am not over fond of any fruit except melons."

That he had a complex relationship with radishes:
"I first of all found that radishes agreed with me; then they did not; now they do again."

That he ate too fast:
"In my haste I often bite my tongue and occasionally my fingers."

—Alain de Botton, *The Consolations of Philosophy*

———

I have remembered, I suppose, what I wanted to remember; many ridiculous things for no reason that makes sense. That is the way we human creatures are made.

—*Agatha Christie: An Autobiography*

———

Begins fervent exploration of all forms that nonfiction takes,
standard formats such as biography, autobiography, interviews,
charts, how a private eye would write a character profile, criminal
background checks, character analysis, etc. . . .

———

This search leads to scrutinizing the ultimate nonfiction entity:
the encyclopedia. Needs to study a typical entry.
Grabs one volume randomly from her office,
places it on bed to read that night.
Volume E.

———

Opens to Einstein's entry. Finishes Einstein, keeps reading,
comes to entry for the word *encyclopedia* itself. Is immediately
intrigued by the history of the encyclopedia, how it evolved,
all the different forms it's taken over the years. It occurs to her
in a moment she feels she will remember always but perhaps
that is just the drama and delusion kicking in:

*I am not writing a memoir (I have no story); I am not writing an autobiography
(for who really cares). I am writing a personal encyclopedia, a thorough
documentation of an ordinary life in the end of the twentieth century/ beginning
of the twenty-first. And in fact, while I didn't know it then, I started this
encyclopedia nearly two years ago, when I began gathering my columns/writings
and putting them in alphabetical order. And I began it even before that, when I
was busy making charts and tables for no apparent reason. And I began it even
before that . . .*

———

As if to lay claim to them, to make sure she is reading it right,
begins typing out these revelatory passages from the entry for
"Encyclopedia." Excitedly nods along, yes, yes, yes,
as the book becomes more and more and more cemented in
her mind, the pieces all finally falling into place.

"... to provide in an orderly arrangement the essence of 'all that is known' on a subject."

"Of the various types of reference works,
the encyclopedia is the only one that can be termed self-contained.
To this end it employs many features that can help in its task,
including illustrations, maps, diagrams, charts, and statistical tables."

"... constructed like an onion, the different layers enclosing the heart."

"Encyclopedias have often reflected fairly accurately the civilization
in which they appeared."

"All great encyclopedia makers have tried to be truthful and to present a
balanced picture of civilization, as they know it, although it is probable that
no encyclopedia is totally unbiased."

"Cross-references are an essential feature of the modern encyclopedia
(system of arrows, or 'see also,' or words in small capital letters which indicate
where additional info can be found)."

"The problem of the encyclopediast has always been to strike the right mean
between too learned and too simplified an approach."

▼

November 2002–March 2003

Gets to work on what she now knows is titled
Encyclopedia of an Ordinary Life

———

Writes, writes.

▼

March 2003

Completes first draft of *Encyclopedia of an Ordinary Life.*
Gives to Charise, family, and agent Amy Rennert.

▼

April/May 2003

Receives valuable feedback from colleagues
John Green, Cynthia Kaplan, Tony Rogers, Dena Fischer.

▼

July 2003

Completes second draft. Sends manuscript to agent.

▼

August 6, 2003

Reads about Jeffrey Middleton, man who has illustrated
new edition of *Webster's Dictionary.*
His style would be perfect for *Encyclopedia*, she thinks.
Tears out article, puts in her book box, just in case, who knows.

▼

September 19, 2003

A handful of editors receive *Encyclopedia of an Ordinary Life* manuscript.

▼

September 23, 2003

First rejection officially comes in.
Here we go.

▼

September 24, 2003

Agent calls to relay positive message she received from an editor in the middle of night. With news that this editor *gets* it, gets intention behind book, AKR feels equipped to handle any outcome from here.

▼

Thursday, October 2, 2003

Book goes to auction. Amy Rennert calls back and forth with updates.
Spends afternoon with Charise.
At six P.M., on way to pick up son Miles from friend's house, receives call from Amy Rennert. It's official.
Crown will be publishing this book. Annik La Farge editor.
Call Jason. Call parents.

▼

9:30 A.M. EST, October 15, 2003
Amy Rosenthal (no relation) and Amy Rosenthal
(no relation), both of New York City, show up at offices of
Crown/Random House on AKR's behalf,
bearing purple irises as a thank-you for editor Annik La Farge.
AKR had discovered the two Amy Rosenthals earlier in the
month through a simple Google search, and after a couple
e-mails and phone conversations explaining
performance thank you concept, the women amazingly
and generously agreed to participate.

▼

February 12, 2004
Jeffrey Middleton agrees to illustrate.

▼

March 1, 2004
Hands in third draft of manuscript.

▼

April 2004
Book goes into production.

▼

May 2004
Sales meetings, publicity meetings.

▼

June 7, 2004
Hands in fourth draft of manuscript.

▼

June 2004/January 2005
Crown people get busy.
Brian Belfiglio, Amy Boorstein, Tina Constable, Lauren Dong,
Meg Drislane, Emily Eilertson, Jill Flaxman, Alison Forner,
Jenny Frost, Doug Jones, Linda Kaplan, Kristin Kiser,
Annik La Farge, Philip Patrick, Dan Rembert, Mario Rojas,
Steve Ross, Karin Schulze, Penny Simon, Barbara Sturman,
and Elizabeth Van Itallie.

▼

November 2004
Book goes to printer.

▼

January 2005
Book gets shipped to warehouses and bookstores.

▼

This moment now
You are here.

X

[pause]

ALPHABETIZED
EXISTENCE

A

AMY

For a while I wished my name was spelled Aimee; it seemed so much more original, innovative, so chock-full of vowels. I like that my name can spell May and yam. When I was growing up, my parents would sing the old song "Once in Love with Amy." I always liked when they did that. In my dating years, the song was "Amie," by Pure Prairie League. Boy: (singing) "Amie / What you wanna do?" I always liked that little serenade as well. The Japanese word *amai* means *the feeling of being cherished and expectation to be loved.* The amygdala is the emotional center of the brain. People close to me call me Aim, and that feels affection-

The amygdala acts as the store-house of emotional memory. Without the amygdala, life is stripped of personal meaning; all passion depends on it.

ate and validating; conversely, I am wary of people I've just met who are prematurely chummy and refer to me that way.

I've been signing my name like this

since the summer after seventh grade, when I invented it at overnight camp sitting on my top bunk.

School assignment, first grade.

Amy Rosenthal

My father-in-law informed me that my married name could produce these two anagrams: Hearty Salmon. Nasty Armhole. I cannot tell you how much I love that.

Answering Machine

In most cases, it is more satisfying to get a friend's answering machine and leave a cheery, tangible trace of your sincere commitment to the friendship than it is to engage in actual conversation.

Anxious, Things That Make Me

Table
TRAIN SCHEDULES
I have to look real close at the columns and small type, and keep double-checking it, as I could be misreading a departure time; a centimeter to the left or right and you're in the entirely wrong little box/column. Even after I've confirmed that there's an 8:06 leaving Chicago's Northwestern Station, I'll pull the crinkly little schedule out of my bag and check one more time. And then, as the final coup de grâce, I'll turn to some guy waiting on the platform and ask, "You're waiting for the 8:06, right?"
VENDING MACHINES
Again, I have to double-, triple-check. *Okay, it's A5 for the Bugles. Is that right? A5?* I don't want to read the codes wrong and end up with the Flaming Hot Cheetos. But then, what a relief when the Bugles tumble down. *Yes! I knew it was A5!*

(continued)

Table (continued)

BIBLIOGRAPHIES

All those commas. Last name of author, comma. First name, comma. Then name of book, underlined. Name of publisher, not underlined. Page numbers, then period. Or is it comma? Writing the paper itself was difficult but manageable. But that bibliography always made my body clench up. To be in that hyperconcentrated mode was nerve-racking. The whole time I'm picturing my teacher reading it, looking for a misplaced comma, eager to tarnish my hard work with red pen marks.

RUNNING INTO SOMEONE

It could be someone I know rather well—an old work colleague, a second cousin—but for some reason I panic and completely blank on their name, and then, at the last possible heart-racing second, the name will come to me.

ALLOTTING ENOUGH TIME TO MAKE FLIGHT

I always work backward. *Okay, the flight leaves at 11:15, so I should be at the airport at 9:15. That means I should leave the house at 8:30—no, play it safe, could be a lot of traffic, say 8:15. That means I need to get up at 7:30; that gives me 45 minutes to get ready and finish any last-minute packing.* As soon as I've come to this conclusion, I'll immediately repeat the whole internal dialogue-calculations, see if I come up with the same time estimates. I'll do this at least a couple more times the day before I leave, one of the times being that night when I set my alarm clock.

APPROACHERS

People are either approachers or avoiders. Approachers will dart across a crowded room and enthusiastically state the obvious: "Oh, my God. It's you! We went to camp together!

I haven't seen you since we were ten!" An avoider, in the same situation, would make no effort whatsoever to reconnect. They reason: *So we once knew each other. That in and of itself is not interesting. I have no desire to acknowledge that we once, long ago, roasted marshmallows together. It will only be awkward to make small talk, and our shared campfire history is of no consequence. I see you. And you see me. That is enough.* And while the avoider *chooses* not to approach, the approacher really has no conscious choice in the matter; approaching is just what they do.

As

As self-conscious as rearranging what's on your coffee table before guests arrive—putting *Art Forum* and Milan Kundera's latest novel on top of *People* magazine and *The Berenstain Bears Potty Book.*

As specific as a mosquito bite on a pinky toe knuckle.

As startling as coming home from vacation and seeing yourself in your own bathroom mirror and only then realizing just how tan you really are.

As out of place as a heap of snow that remains by a street lamp on a sunny April day long after all the other snow has melted.

Ayn Rand

Ayn Rand seems so mysterious, privy, snobby—in a cool way. I'm pretty sure it's the *y*.

See also: Letters

B

BAD MOVIE

Upon hearing that a friend of mine saw a bad movie, a movie I knew would be bad and never would have gone to see myself, I think, *Of course that movie sucked. How could you have thought it wouldn't? You are sheeplike to have gone to see it in the first place. This is definitely going to affect our friendship.*

See also: Calling Someone's Name; Smooth Jazz

BAGPIPERS

They have hired bagpipers to play at the wedding. There are two of them, in full Scottish regalia, standing in the field playing. It is a most unusual image, these two men in kilts by a tree, performing for us. Even more startling is how, after only five minutes or so, we are used to them. There is nothing unusual about them anymore; they are now part of the scenery, nothing more, nothing less. I imagine if they started hurling eggplants at each other, we would, in no time, mentally readjust and be rather ho-hum about it.

BIRTHDAY

I like my birthday, the actual date April 29—it seems right, like it matches me, the capital *A* of April, the way the number 29 feels, the whole spring flavor. I am very glad I was born and definitely appreciate the ongoing alive status that each birthday brings, but I do not typically get into the animated birthday hoopla spirit. I do recognize, however, that for me it is a fine line between not wanting to make a big deal about my birthday but also wanting family and certain friends to dote enough to satisfy some nebulous quality/quantity acknowledged-my-birthday barometer. When I was a kid, my mom always made sure my brother and sisters and I woke up to birthday signs and her famous Krouse Klown drawing. I tried instating the Rosenthal Rabbit for my own kids, but it fizzled out because in my mind it never felt as special or as important as the Krouse Klown; it felt fraudulent and satirical. For as many April 29s as I can remember, my mom has presented me with a poem, a tender, rhyming summary of my life up to that point, and it is these gifts of verse written in her lovely Ann Krouse script that are the centerpiece of each birthday.

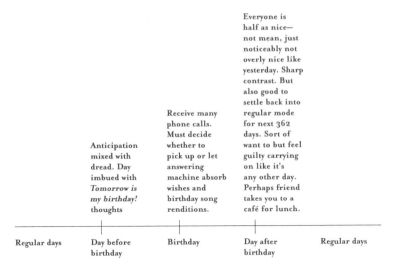

Regular days	Day before birthday	Birthday	Day after birthday	Regular days
	Anticipation mixed with dread. Day imbued with *Tomorrow is my birthday!* thoughts	Receive many phone calls. Must decide whether to pick up or let answering machine absorb wishes and birthday song renditions.	Everyone is half as nice— not mean, just noticeably not overly nice like yesterday. Sharp contrast. But also good to settle back into regular mode for next 362 days. Sort of want to but feel guilty carrying on like it's any other day. Perhaps friend takes you to a café for lunch.	

BIRTHMARK

I have a birthmark on my left arm. As a child I thought it looked like a bear, or Africa, depending on the angle. I would often draw an eye and a mouth on it; sometimes I would allow a friend to do so. To look at my birthmark was to remind myself that I was me.

BLUSH

I blush easily.

BOWLING

It would be difficult to convince me that leaning has no effect whatsoever on the outcome of my bowling.

BOZO CIRCUS

My husband and I were out with another couple—two messy-haired, way-smarter-than-us professor types. It came up that one of their friends had just won the Nobel Prize. *You guys actually know someone who won the Nobel Prize?! That's amazing*, I said. In a matter-of-fact way, they added, *Actually, we seem to know about twenty or so people who have won a Nobel Prize. Well*, I said, *I have never won the Nobel Prize, but when I was four, I was picked for the Grand Prize Game on* Bozo Circus. They were incredulous. *God! What was it like? I always wanted to be on that show.* For them, the Nobel Prize, while a nice honor, no longer loomed as the powerful end-all. But my brush with Bozo—now, that was really something. I told them all about the magic arrows; how I made it to bucket number three; and that I had walked away with a year's supply of pudding, an Archie board game, and panty hose for my mom.

BRODSKY, JOSEPH

I have just started Joseph Brodsky's book *On Grief and Reason*. Let me say I have only read one essay in a collection of thirty, and I flipped through the book, sizing up the chapters, actually counting the pages, 1, 2, 3, 4, 5, 6, 7—yes, this one's good, it only has seven pages. This hardly counts as being familiar with

Joseph Brodsky, reading seven pages and the jacket bio, yet I can tell you that his essay *In Praise of Boredom* is one of the best things I have ever read; that I think you would be stimulated and moved by it; that I'd be happy to direct you to a copy of it; and that I now know this of Brodsky: he really liked Robert Frost. He was particularly infatuated with the line *The only way out is through.* He quoted it in this one essay, and then when I flipped through the book looking for another essay I wasn't intimidated by, I found the same quote again.

That's how it is. That's how it always is. In a handful of pages we can see a writer's defining twitch: One has a fondness for ellipses; one constantly references his *jumpiness* (Thurber); another fancies single-word sentences; another has a sloppy habit of overusing the word *surprisingly;* still another leans on a Robert Frost quote. Perhaps Brodsky never thought the two essays, which contained that reference, would end up in a bound volume. (One would have hoped the editor would have picked up on this, and at least separated the essays more substantially. It's tragic really. When my work is left to be poked through, will it be painfully obvious that I gravitated toward semicolons, and frequently wrote about coincidences and doughnuts with sprinkles?) If Brodsky used that quote in those two essays, we can be sure he brought it up at dinner parties; at a literary conference in Turin; over coffee with an old chum from the University of Michigan.

Right now I think his book will change my life. Brodsky makes me feel alive. He seems to know things. His knowing will allow *me* to know. He will beam me to a higher place—a place that's vaguely different, sharper, where the dial's been shifted just a notch to the right (that's all it took!) and everything clicked into place.

This happens to be my immediate reaction every time someone or something truly gets me. I think, *Oh, this new book/new friend/new sweater will alter the course of my life in a profound way.* It was like that even when I was young, with a small box. I remember the power of receiving a certain small keepsake box. I excitedly put all my things in it, all the things that mattered to me, all the things that had meaning; nothing mattered anymore but what was in that box. But then after one, two, maybe four days tops, I grew tired of the box, or the hinge broke, or my disloyalty made itself evident when I chose not to take it to a sleepover at Rosalie Press's house. Any number of scenarios may have occurred that ultimately led to the same feeling of disenchantment. Brodsky is my new box.

BROKEN

The CD player in our kitchen causes the first three songs to skip. The CD player in the baby's room no longer functions at all, although up until recently, at least the radio worked. I've broken every computer I've ever owned. My current printer and fax programs are incompatible. I jam the Xerox machine nearly every time I touch it. I go through Walkmans like paper towels.

The screen on our back porch is so badly ripped that the kids don't even bother opening the actual door, they simply lift the big, detached flap and walk right through it. The children's bathtub drain is partially clogged with small toys; actually, there is no real drain there—it was broken years ago and now we compensate by stuffing a washcloth in there, every single night. Their double stroller has snapped in half.

There are long black wires hanging from the ceiling in my office because we still haven't installed the lights and fans. The fan light in the master bedroom never once worked. The light switch in the baby's room has never once worked. Our beautiful antique chair in the family room has had visibly broken springs for half a year now. I just noticed that one of the handlebars on my treadmill fell off. The boys broke my favorite barrette. I broke the glass serving dish with the decorative dolphin trim. We do not have a single glass left from our bridal registry.

BROKER

It is weird and unsettling that a person who is hired to handle your money, make wise decisions about it, and, ostensibly, keep you from losing it is called a broker.

BROTHER

My brother, who grew up with three sisters, was I won't say how many years old when he finally realized that he did not have to wrap the towel around his chest when he came out of the shower.

BUSY

How you been?
Busy.

How's work?
Busy.

How was your week?
Good. Busy.

You name the question, "*Busy*" is the answer. Yes, yes, I know we are all terribly busy doing terribly important things. But I think more often than not, "*Busy*" is simply the most acceptable knee-jerk response.

Certainly there are more interesting, more original, and more accurate ways to answer the question *how are you?* How about: *I'm hungry for a waffle; I'm envious of my best friend; I'm annoyed by everything that's broken in my house; I'm itchy.*

Yet *busy* stands as the easiest way of summarizing all that you do and all that you are. *I am busy* is the short way of saying—suggesting—my time is filled, my phone does not stop ringing, and you (therefore) should think well of me.

Have people always been this busy? Did cavemen think they were busy, too? *This week is crazy—I've got about ten caves to draw on. Can I meet you by the fire next week?* I have a hunch that there is a direct correlation between the advent of coffee chains and the increase in busy-ness. Look at us. We're all pros now at hailing a cab/pushing a grocery cart/operating a forklift with a to-go cup in hand. We're skittering about like hyperactive gerbils, high not just on caffeine but on caffeine's luscious by-product, productivity. Ah, the joy of doing, accomplishing, crossing off.

As kids, our stock answer to most every question was *nothing. What did you do at school today? Nothing. What's new? Nothing.* Then, somewhere on the way to adulthood, we each took a 180-degree turn. We cashed in our *nothing* for *busy.*

I'm starting to think that, like youth, the word *nothing* is wasted on the young. Maybe we should try reintroducing it into our grown-up vernacular. *Nothing.* I say it a few times and I can feel myself becoming more quiet, decaffeinated. *Nothing.* Now I'm picturing emptiness, a white blanket, a couple ducks gliding on a still pond. *Nothing. Nothing. Nothing.* How did we get so far from it?

See also: Coffee, Stopping for;
Crossing Guard; Nothing

BUTTERFLY

Once you learn how to draw a butterfly, you just want to keep doing it. There is something calming and satisfying about drawing them. Maybe it has to do with the symmetry, and the curves of the wings.

BUTTERSCOTCH

I love butterscotch but rarely think to seek it out.

C

CAB OF TRUCK

Seeing just the short, truncated nubby front part of a semi-truck (the cab), one is always compelled to point and say *look*. It's just an image you can't get used to. It registers in the brain as funny, odd, on the loose.

CALLING SOMEONE'S NAME

You're calling someone's name, trying to get their attention. Perhaps you're in a crowd. Or they are across the street. Or they went to get popcorn and Raisinets and are now looking for you in the packed movie theater. You cup your hands around your mouth and repeatedly call their name, waving your arm—*Here I am*—but they don't hear or see you. No matter who they are—a lawyer, a surgeon, a Latin scholar—they look like an idiot searching for you, craning their head like that, and you question their intelligence.

See also: Bad Movie; Smooth Jazz

CAPRICIOUS

I kept a vocabulary journal for a while in my early twenties. I had just added the words *capricious* and *precarious* to the list, and while talking to Brian on the phone, I decided to try them out. I said something about life being both *capricious* and *precarious*. Knowing me as he did, he immediately picked up this finagled repertoire—my God, I myself could practically see the neon arrows flashing as each word slipped out into the air. *Oooooh, fancy words, Amy,* he said. I more or less ignored the comment, as a way of implying that I didn't think one way or the other about these words, that they were just the kinds of bon mots I used all the time now, no biggie. I wished the words would have felt more worn in in my mouth, the way words do after you've said them hundreds of time. *Table. Melt. Floundering.* See, I can say any of those without thinking about them as I say them. But he, Brian, had spotted capricious' and precarious' stiffness; in fact, he caught me with the tags on. I think of this every time I use or hear either of those words.

[Aside]
I added the Capricious entry on the afternoon of April 15, 2003.
Later that night, I received an e-mail from Brian.
I had not spoken to him in eight years.

CAR

When I'm in my car and someone lets me in their lane and I not only mouth *Thank you* to the other driver, but I actually say it out loud—as if they could hear me—I am taken aback, it sounded so goofy, hearing my voice alone in my car.

CAR RADIO

. . . and when you get back in the car, the loudness of the radio startles you. It didn't seem so loud before because you turned it up gradually throughout the ride.

Table

SOUNDS THAT ARE LOUD THOUGH QUIET

▶ A mosquito buzzing in your camping tent at three A.M.

(continued)

► A phone that should be ringing but is not.

► Sitting in the waiting room waiting for a medical procedure and then hearing the nurse call your name.

► The snipping of scissors cutting your long hair short.

► The crunching of sitting on your sunglasses.

► The first time he/she whispers "*I love you.*"

► Your four-year-old saying something inappropriate in front of your mother, or someone you hoped would be especially taken with your child and parenting skills.

► Someone who won't stop drumming their fingers or tapping their pen on the table.

► Your pee when you're in the stall next to your boss.

► The unwrapping of a small piece of candy in a place of worship.

CAR WASH

Every time I go to my local car wash, the owner peers inside, throws his arms up, and says, *Oh, Miss—very dirty. Very, very dirty.* I'm sorry. I didn't know I was supposed to bring it in clean.

CATCH

David threw a crumpled-up piece of paper to me. I caught it, looked at it, then set it down. He then threw a paper clip. Again, I caught it, put it down. *Come on, Amy. Don't you get it?! Throw it back!* he yelled. How was I supposed to know that was what he wanted? I am a girl. I do not have the catch gene. Guys have the catch gene. That is why the symbol for male is ♂. It stands for *throw the ball.*

CD, New

I love the moment when I get a new CD and it holds the promise of being the best CD ever—all that potential, so many good songs to fall in love with, the dense liner notes to inspect. But then I realize, This song's not so great, neither's the next one— ew, what's with that harmonica solo?—and in the end I like maybe two songs, love one, and within a few days it disappears under a stack of other loose, orphaned CDs. And going back to those two or three favorite songs—I feel bad listening to them exclusively, that's somehow cheating. I must listen to the CD in its entirety, to not play favorites so to speak, and when those killer tunes come on, well, I've earned the privilege fair and square. This is not unlike my policy of occasionally rotating my least favorite jeans into the mix—*There. I wore them. Happy?*—and feeling justified the next morning in resorting once again to my beloved worn-in pair.

Chain Letters

I despise chain letters. They were amusing once, in third grade. But now I resent the intrusion, the assumption that I will play along, the CAPITAL-LETTER THREATS of what will happen to me if I don't. When they used to arrive by regular mail, I had a kind of oh geesh reaction; I would feel disappointed in my friend, misunderstood: Doesn't she know the first thing about me? Doesn't she know I hate this and that I find it void of meaning, credibility, and beauty? But now when I get these forwarded chain letters in my e-mail, I don't really feel agitated—I can and do simply delete them in a split second—I feel baffled. Does my friend really have time for this? Does she really believe this? I picture her at her computer, clicking on her address book, wasting minutes from her too-short-as-it-is life.

CHANGE

> *This money was left here intentionally and is specifically for your use. I know it's not much—perhaps just enough to treat yourself to a cookie, coffee, a lottery ticket, donation to the homeless, a new pair of socks. . . . In any case, I hope it changes your day for the better. All I ask in return is that you let me know how you spend it. You don't have to sign your name, and a prepaid postcard is included. Enjoy.*

Every week, for close to a year, I left an envelope containing this note, some loose change, and a stamped postcard addressed to my P.O. box for a random stranger to discover. I'd like to say that I set out to do this for purely altruistic reasons. But, more accurately, I did it because I'm easily bored/easily amused, and experiments such as this inject a morsel of suspense into the week. That, and I really like getting mail.

It was always fun to plan where to leave the envelopes. I sent a few with friends traveling out of town. I left them in phone booths, taxis, and newspaper boxes. I left them on sidewalks, airplanes, and restaurant tables. I left them at a bookstore, a doctor's office, and a bar mitzvah. Once, at a jazz bar, I watched a bride go into the bathroom, so I casually slipped in behind her and strategically left the envelope for her by the sink. She ran out, waving the envelope and screaming *Look at this!* to her bridal party. That was a highlight. Though I never did hear from her.

I got ten postcards back. I was always amazed when I got a response. And I was always amazed when I didn't. Responding was nearly effortless, yet most people apparently couldn't be bothered. I couldn't help but obsess over this: Did the postcard just get lost in a pile somewhere? Do they vow daily, *I'm definitely going to mail this today,* but somehow never get around to it? Did they think it was creepy—that they were being followed, or that by mailing the postcard they could be traced? Did they—those slimes—peel the stamp off the postcard for their own use?

I'd like to think that how the ten people who returned their cards chose to spend their change said something (profound?) about them, in the same way that whatever poster you hung over your bed in college offered visitors an assessment of Who You Really Are. The responses ranged from the American Dream—"Florida Lottery Ticket for $55 million"—to Zen simplicity—"Bought a piece of fresh fruit."

Two spoke of serendipity:

I was walking down North Avenue on June 12 (my birthday), had a fight with my partner, and almost flat broke. I chose to walk down North Avenue because several years ago that street was somewhat inspirational for me and I was thinking, "I dig North Ave." I met a sweet woman on the street who needed some money—gave it to her. She offered me a beer to celebrate my day—I declined. What an Oprah Winfrey move—you sure you're not Oprah? Anyhow, thanks for the smile.

And this from Helen, the woman who works in the locker room at my health club:

Hello. I'm sorry; I forgot to write for you how I spend money. I found money in locker Sunday when I forgot my money for breakfast. I opened and say thanks God and thanks for you. Helen, Lake Shore Club (you see me in club please).

There was the philanthropist:

Donated to Amy Erickson Alternative Cancer Treatment Fund.

And the realist:

Thank you for the gift! I added it to my fabulous coin collection, which I keep in an apple cider bottle and which I'll use to partially finance my upcoming move. Thanks again for your thoughtful offering. Every little bit does help out and it's so fun to receive help from a stranger.

I gave away between fifty cents and $1.50 each week. In the end, that probably added up to about sixty bucks counting the postage—the amount Bill Gates leaves in those penny dishes by the register. But if a few people got a kick out of it, I'm hoping the mighty karma gods who saw me bite Bobby Bycraft in first grade will now call it a wash. Plus, as I say, I got mail.

Cheek Bouncing

I was flipping through the Sunday *Magazine* and came across an article about a fraudulent high-society woman. Let me see if I can retrace exactly what happened from there. 1. I glanced at the photo. 2. I then glanced over at the headline . . . *Caused a Stir in New York Society This Year.* 3. Ouch. Good juicy gossip, I thought. 4. Back to headline: *Especially When Her Cheeks Started Bouncing.* 5. *What, her cheeks were bouncing? What's up with that?* 6. Look back at photo. *Well, she certainly does have big cheeks. Maybe she had some freaky plastic surgery? And now her cheeks jiggle in a strange way, especially noticeable when she struts into high-society events? Perhaps her cheeks are full of silicon? She could be some kind of spy, in disguise? Or maybe she's fake, like a robot person?* 7. I reread the headline: checks, her *checks* were bouncing. *Okay, that makes a lot more sense.* 8. I proceeded to show the article to my husband and my friend John, and strangely enough, they both read it the same way. *Cheeks started bouncing,* they'd say, and kinda chuckle snort. It must be something about the smiling, cheeky photo that triggers the brain to read the second *c* in *checks* as an *e* (and they *are* very similar-looking letters to begin with, even more so in the *New York Times*'s typeface). I'm pretty certain that without the photo, there wouldn't be any confusion with the cheek/check headline.

See also: Farmer; Words That Look Similar

Chef Hat

Surely they can design more flattering chef hats.

Chicago Fire

Justin (age six): We saw the Chicago Fire on our field trip.

Me: You did? You mean, you saw something about it down-town?

Justin: No, Mom. You don't understand. The Chicago Fire is a statue.

Me: I see. You know, Justin, I think you missed the Chicago Fire part of your class when you were sick last week.

Justin: The Chicago Fire was last week?

Childhood Memories

Chronology of Events

1965
Amy Krouse is born, April 29.

1967
Amy's sister Beth is born, October 16.

1968
Beth is in crib. Amy asks if she is thirsty. Pours glass of water on Beth's head.

1969–1977
When Amy is home sick, her mother rubs her back while taking her temperature and sings the song she always sings when Amy is not feeling well. She sings so nice and soft.

I'm a little doll that has just been broken,
Fallen from my mommy's knees.
I'm a little doll that has just been broken,
Won't you love me please?

1969

Goes to Kiddie Kollege for preschool. ————————

1970

*Amy's brother, Joe, is born December 16, two and a
half months prematurely.*

1970

*Practices swimming in pool with father. She starts on stairs, he stands wait-
ing a few feet away. Just as she approaches him, he takes a step back.
He keeps doing this. He is encouraging about it, but she is nervous, out
of breath. Doesn't want to keep going, doesn't want to be pushed to limit,
feels misled—Don't do that!—just wants to be swept up in his arms
when she reaches him. The relief, the snugness, the glory, of finally being
in Dad's safe arms.*

1970–1974

*Gets to stir father's coffee. Watches the cream change the color to light
brown.*

1970–1975

*Father occasionally comes home from work with box of Jujubes as
special treat.*

1970–1980

*Gets to pick out a Dum Dum lollipop from the bottom file-cabinet
drawer after every visit to nice, bald pediatrician Dr. Nachman.
Typically chooses butterscotch flavor; hates the root-beer one.*

1970–1980

Amy falls asleep in car on way home from trip downtown or dinner at relatives' house. Remarkable to her that she awakes just as they enter her subdivision, a minute from home. Seems to Amy that she has a talent for knowing precisely how long to sleep, exactly when to wake up. Not until she is older does she realize it was the motion of going fast on the highway that lulled her to sleep, that the car's slowing down on small neighborhood streets was what stirred her awake.

1970–1980

Amy is served chicken pot pie when her parents go out on Saturday night. Steaming-hot cream sauce scorches roof of her mouth.

1971

Amy invents a game with sister Beth: Ooga. Ooga It. Odd sort of running game with rules that are unspoken, nonsensical, and completely adhered to. They play it for hours, screaming, "Ooga! Ooga it!"

1971–1979

Amy watches parents slow-dance in kitchen. Covers face with hands. Feels embarrassed but happy.

1971

First grade. In music class with Mrs. Swanson. Amy by mistake adds extra syllable to remember, *says* rememember. *When their teacher Mrs. Stern comes to pick up the class, Mrs. Swanson asks Amy to say* rememember *again for Mrs. Stern. They both think it's so cute. Amy feels that reenactment is strangely forced but likes the attention.*

1971

Overhears mother on phone saying, "I think this summer I am going to send Amy to C-A-M-P," *and figures out what it spells.*

1971

Takes turns showing privates with boy across street in his wooded back-yard. Feels odd, devious, interesting. Recognizes that exposed genitals emit certain energy. In the end, feels she has been swayed. Glad when he later moves away.

1971

Steve C., a boy in her grade, dies in a car accident. Seems unreal, spooky. Haunted by idea of him gone. Thinks about him, the absence of this once–alive boy, for rest of life.

1971–1972

Amy goes to Florida to see grandmother. Grandmother's friend Gladys has them to dinner. Radishes on the salad—Amy tries for the first time and loves them. Flurry of comments about radishes, older women say how unusual it is for child to like radishes. Year later, Amy returns. Again they have dinner at Gladys's. Again Gladys serves radishes, now in Amy's honor. These radishes taste different—bitter, sharp, stinging. Amy confused; other radishes so sweet. But Gladys served them especially for her, remembered how much she loved them. Amy doesn't have heart or courage to speak up; forces herself to eat radishes.

1972

Amy rubs her stomach real lightly until she gets goose bumps. Puts her in a trance.

1972

Amy realizes one night at dinner that ribs are ribs, as in ribs like people have ribs, ribs are the ribs of an animal.

Table

WHAT MY CHILDHOOD TASTED LIKE

Item	Notes
Fruit cocktail on top of cottage cheese	Liked the grapes and maraschino cherries
Marinated flank steak	Liked the dark, crispy stringy ends
Hot dog paprikosh	Especially good with very cold applesauce
Barbecue ribs	Mesmerized by my mom gnawing on bones
Heart-shaped hamburgers	What my mom made on Valentine's Day
M&M's	Always in the candy dish on Thanksgiving
Parsley	Dipped in salt water at Passover seder
Homemade cheesecake w/ strawberry topping	Picking at leftovers in the fridge, chunks of the graham cracker crust, that aluminum tin
Triscuits	Endless handfuls
Slice of American cheese	The one thing we were allowed to eat before dinner; everything else would apparently "spoil our appetite"
Grand Marnier soufflé	What my parents were baking late one night; I woke up for some reason and was allowed to stay up with them and help. Very big deal, very special treat. Felt like I was really in on something cool, as my other three sibs slept upstairs. This soufflé thing seemed very exotic, grown-up. Seemed like midnight. Was probably 9 P.M.

(continued)

Table (continued)

WHAT MY CHILDHOOD TASTED LIKE

Item	Notes
Bazooka gum	The idea of "allowing six to eight weeks for delivery" on all Bazooka Joe prizes seemed like an unimaginable eternity.
Baskin-Robbins mint chocolate chip ice cream cake	Hated mint and was always disappointed when the mom walked out with it at birthday parties.
Swiss cheese appetizer	What my mom made at all holidays. Loved it. Recipe: Mix together ½ pound grated Swiss cheese, 1 small grated onion, 3–4 tablespoons mayonnaise (enough to moisten). Place Pinahs Original Crunchy Bread Chips on cookie sheet. Spread teaspoonful of mixture on each chip. Broil in oven for about 60 seconds or so, keeping an eye on them so they don't burn.
Froot Loops and bubblegum	One of those stories that got told and retold over the years. What I "made" for my parents for their anniversary dinner when I was five years old.
Hawaiian Punch	Super sweet, left tinge of red on upper lips. Came in a big can. Poured it out of two triangle openings on top of can.

1972

Conscious of using for the very first time, albeit only in her mind, a swear word when her mom made her mad.

1972

Amy receives call at school; sister Katie is born, March 22. More excited about unusual occurrence of having principal deliver a message to her classroom than about having new sibling.

1972–1983

Family sings the family song together. Passed down from father's side. Feeling of contentment singing it. Keg/beer reference goes over her head.

> The Krouse family is the best family
> The best family from old Hungary
> Singing glorious, glorious
> One keg of beer for the six of us
> And it's glory be to God that there are no more of us
> Cause one of us could drink it all alone.
> Ba-da-du-dum

1972

Playing at neighbor's, Amy gets a stomachache. From the bathroom, Amy tells Mrs. Bycraft that it hurts bad, her stomach. Mrs. Bycraft tells Amy to cross her arms and hold her stomach tightly, that sometimes helps. Amy does not feel good but is strangely cozy in that little bathroom, with the little window overlooking the backyard.

1972

Amy listens to Helen Reddy eight-track in station wagon. Watches her mother put lipstick on in the rearview mirror.

1972

Jamie Kasova, older girl who lives across street, informs Amy that if you drop your gum on pavement, it is gross to put back in your mouth.

1972–1982

Amy is constantly filled with questions. Life seems extremely confusing, complex, layered. Is sure that adults attend a kind of convention where they are given all the answers, let in on subtle truths. She thinks she will never be able to utter a statement, to speak and not have it be a question. Idea of saying something in the affirmative seems unfathomable.

1973

Amy thinks her friend Rosalie Press is lucky because all the seat belt buckles in their car say Press.

1973–1983

Amy loves running her hand under the hot water while her mom takes a bath. They talk.

1973

Amy gets the skin between her thumb and forefinger caught in metal lever after flushing the toilet at school. Too embarrassed to tell teacher, so sits through rest of school with red, throbbing hand. Only thing that seems to relieve pain is putting pinched skin in her mouth and sucking on it. It is cold that day, but when she walks home, she keeps off one mitten so she can suck on injured skin. Arrives home with sore, freezing hand.

1973

Amy and Beth watch The Brady Bunch *in family room, lying on stomachs, heads propped up by elbows, chins resting in cupped hands. They always call who they are for each episode. Amy calls that she is Marcia. Beth must be Jan or Cindy.*

Family room of childhood home.

1973

Amy relays to her mother part of story she is reading. Mother corrects her with a smile: The girl's name is pronounced with a soft g, *Ginny. Amy realizes she has read nearly the entire book saying Ginny with a hard* g *in her mind. She is standing in corner of family room at the time, her mother sitting in red chair.*

1973

Each morning leading up to Nixon's impeachment, Amy waits for her father to read newspaper headlines, then asks whether Nixon is impeached yet. Has only the vaguest sense of what **impeach** *means. While she knows enough to know it has nothing to do with peaches, it is still the image that comes to mind.*

1973

Amy returns from being out sick and takes a make-up spelling test with Mrs. Gotchalk. Misspells **coat** *even though she knows how to spell* **coat**, *of course she knows how to spell* **coat**. *Feels chagrin.*

1973

On hot summer days, pulls bottom of T-shirt up through neck and down, making a sort of midriff-baring halter top. Will have flirtatious undertones in later years, but for now, totally innocent gesture.

1973

Mrs. Bycraft tells Amy that they are moving. Amy panics, asks Mrs. Bycraft if she'll still be here for Amy's birthday, as if that is all that matters.

1974

Trades Wacky Packages cards with friends.

1974

Amy writes a letter to PBS. Tells them she wants to have her own TV show. Outlines what it would be like. Hopes they don't notice the obvious **Zoom** *similarities.*

1974

Amy sits at the school lunch table and talks about what the class has just learned in science that morning, something about the effect warm water has on the body, how it makes some people have to go to the bathroom. She blurts out, "Oh, yeah—that's why I always have to pee in the bathtub!" *She waits for everyone else to say,* "I do that, too," *but no one does. Mortified, but also knows she could not have not said it, understands that it is her nature to reveal this sort of thing.*

1974

Amy's father drops a can of shaving cream on his toe. Rather severe injury for a toe. Big deal in their house.

1974

Amy badly hurts leg at playground, on tornado slide. Game entails sitting horizontally midway down slide and with outstretched legs trying to block friends from getting past. Weight of kids sends Amy down slide but right leg remains stuck in mass of bodies. Leg twists and snaps. Then Amy passes out. This becomes a story she will now tell throughout her life. On crutches for long time. Gets special desk at school, in corner, against far left wall, so she can keep leg elevated on chair. Is allowed to decorate her space, tack something up on wall next to her. Very exciting. Imagines this must be what it's like to have own apartment, one's own space.

1974

Amy gets a shirt for her birthday that says Amy *on the front and* 9 *on the back. One of her favorite presents ever. Wears it all the time. Asks for a* 10 *shirt on next birthday. Gets it, but it is different, not same soft material, stiffer. Stays in her drawer. First (but not last) lesson about futility of trying to replicate good thing or good experience—never as good second time, only causes disappointment.*

Amy/9 shirt.

1975

Amy is hanging out at her parents' office—which is in her family's basement at the time—talking to an employee, Cathy. Amy wants to show Cathy a game she learned at school. Amy sings "Yankee Doodle Dandy," but with each word starting with F. *Fankee foodle fent fo fown . . .*

She gets to joke point of the song—fuck a feather. *Cathy not amused. Amy feels ashamed, remorseful. Tries to back-pedal. Unconvincingly says she did not know about bad part, thought joke was word* phony . . . fiding on a phony.

1975
Fourth grade. Can't quite figure out what the word mandatory *means. Teacher often uses it when talking about homework and in-class projects, but Amy is confused: Is that the one that means it's optional, so you don't have to do it, or the one that means you absolutely have to do it? Too far into school year to ask about it.*

1975–1983
Amy gets a strange echo sensation in her head, a state that comes over her out of nowhere. She is sitting on floor on side of her bed, facing closet. Tries to concentrate on this pounding inner echo; seems to amplify her thoughts as if over loudspeaker with reverb. Tries to make sense of it. Maybe something wrong with her brain? Sits it out, waits for it to dissipate; it does after a few minutes. This happens several times throughout her childhood.

1975
Amy and friends sing McDonald's jingle as fast as they can: Two all-beef patties, special sauce, lettuce, cheese, pickles, onions, on a sesame seed bun.

1975
Asked to sit down on parents' bed, something to tell her. It's early morning, before school. Parents say that her friend M. will need her more than ever today. Bad things about M.'s father on news and in newspaper. Had hired someone to kill his wife. Got caught. In jail. Thinks of lanky, longhaired M. down the street. Enormity of incident felt at this moment, but soon rumors migrate, school is still school, M. is still M., and succession of regular days wears down episode's coarse edges.

1975

Susie Rabyne's dad is driving Amy and Susie home from somewhere. They are on highway. He points to road sign: INDIANA, NEXT EXIT. *He says,* What do you say, guys—should we go to Indiana? *Amy gets excited, sits up on one knee, peeks her head in gap between driver and passenger seat.* Wow! *she thinks.* He's serious! Fantastic spontaneous adventure! We will bypass plain old Chicago and go to Indiana! Indiana—a whole new state! *They come to turnoff; Mr. Rabyne keeps going straight. Amy realizes he was only kidding. Amy is deflated. Untucks her leg and sits back down regular on seat.*

1975

Krouse children are all told they can only watch educational TV, such as news. Learn to quickly switch to news channel when they hear parents walk in front door.

Table	
MOST MEMORABLE TV SHOWS AND MOVIES	
The Carol Burnett Show	The Wizard of Oz
The Flip Wilson Show	Our Town, *play on PBS*
The Brady Bunch	Escape to Witch Mountain
The Electric Company	Forever, *with Stephanie Zimbalist*
Speed Racer	
Schoolhouse Rock	The Other Side of the Mountain
Land of the Lost	
Creature Features	One on One, *with Robby Benson*
James at 15	
The Wonderful World of Disney, *on Sunday nights*	A Little Romance, *with Diane Lane*
Family, *with Kristy McNichol*	Airplane
Zoom	Arthur
Eight Is Enough	Grease
The Love Boat	Fiddler on the Roof
Fantasy Island	

1975

Amy has two major revelations. The first: She discovers people don't just go to work, they have specific jobs. Prior to 1975, Amy assumes everyone does same thing, more or less—aside from policemen, firemen, doctors; only concrete image conjured up for her by word work *is one of grown-up departing from home. She learns that her neighbor Mr. Bycraft works for Dial soap. Job has something to do with producing or wrapping or selling of soap. Fascinating, that there are actually people who do this, though upon reflection it makes complete sense to her. Then learns her uncle is a steel businessman; this apparently involves getting chunks of steel and doing something to it and then selling it to someone. How many kinds of jobs there must be—she imagines dozens for sure.*

The second discovery has to do with filmmaking. Amy thinks that when they make a movie, they film it in sequence, set up each scene in exact order of story. Incredulous at hassle of undertaking: Finish one scene, go to different location (or country!) and shoot that scene, then six scenes and many locations later, back to same place, set it up exact same way again. She now learns about concept of editing, is very relieved.

Table A

THINGS THAT CONFUSED ME FOR MUCH LONGER THAN THEY SHOULD HAVE

How they could have pools on ships. Thought it was just a hole in middle of ship that let in ocean water. Then wouldn't people be left in ocean if ship kept moving?

Horatio Alger—baseball player or famous writer?

Why terrorists would take credit for bombings—why would they admit that?

How coincidental it would be that, say, Sylvester Stallone was on Johnny Carson exactly when *Rambo* came out.

Which ones were the mittens and which ones were the gloves.

(continued)

Table A (continued)

Thought they were saying "ten year," like really good teachers would be granted a ten-year contract. Tenure. Oh. They're saying *tenure*.

Thought they were saying "old-timers" when describing people who were really old and forgetful. I figured they were just speaking fast, slurring the *d* and the *t*, making the word *old-timers* sound like *Alzheimer's*.

What "under new management" meant.

Table B

WHAT MY FRIENDS WERE CONFUSED BY AS CHILDREN

I couldn't understand the difference between a sound track in a movie, which the actors supposedly could not hear, and if there was a radio on in the movie, which the actors could hear. Music would be playing and I'd say to my mom, "Okay, can they hear that? Okay, now can they hear that?"

If it was raining out and a fire truck went racing by, I didn't understand how there could be a fire. If it was raining, I figured the water would just put it out.

I remember seeing construction going on and wondering when everything would be finished—that one day all the construction everywhere would be totally done.

I used to think I could see atoms, but it was just dust.

I couldn't understand how people could be so stupid to die in plane crashes. If they knew the plane was going down, why wouldn't they just jump out on the wing and jump off?

My earliest memory of having a bath with my dad involved him covering up his private parts with a washcloth. When it came time for the discussion about sex with Mom, I thought that a penis looked like a washcloth.

I thought the basement of department stores would fill up with steps from the escalator pushing them down all day.

I thought that when my parents were little the world was in black and white because all the pictures of them were black and white.

We were driving past the hospital once, and my mom said, "That's where you were born." I thought she was pointing at the phone booth on the corner, so for the longest time, whenever I saw someone enter a phone booth, I thought they were going to come out with a baby.

I didn't understand that grandparents were your parents' parents. I just thought that every family got nice, old, unrelated couples assigned to them. They would then bring you presents and come to Sunday dinner. All the other kids had them, too, so I figured it was some kind of rule.

I always got the words pedestrian *and* Presbyterian *confused. I didn't understand why Presbyterians always had the right of way.*

The term gay demonstration *really threw me. I couldn't picture what that would look like. Like do they really demonstrate it?*

I used to think that all men's trousers came with change in them.

Whenever I saw those tiny planes that leave streaks of white in the sky, I thought that it was someone's job to do that. And that's what I wanted to do when I grew up; I thought I would revolutionize the field by drawing more creative things in the sky than just straight lines.

I remember going to the symphony as a child and getting a glimpse of the music on the conductor's stand. I thought the little marks on the page— the notes—were what showed him how he was supposed to move his arms around.

1975

Amy likes Biff Pittman. Last day of fifth grade he gives her note saying he likes her, too. She can't believe it. She is so happy. Amy + Biff = true love forever.

1976

Sixth grade. Biff breaks up with Amy. Confused. Had never thought of the possibility of an ending, concept hadn't occurred to her, had assumed their link was an unchanging, indefinite thing. Devastated.

1976

*Learns the word **gregarious**. Remembers the definition by associating it with her cousin Greg—Greg is Gregarious. From that point on, thinks of the word this way.*

1976

Goes to Fayva shoe store at corner strip mall and steals leather laces from shoes to make friendship bracelets with Rosalie Press and Anne Rogers. Trio also invents Sensational Club. Girls labor over club name and insignia. Very pleased with results.

1976

Ellen comes to work for Krouses. Her hands are weathered and fingers long. Ankles and feet are small for rest of body. Says to Amy, "You're just as cute as you wanna be." Plays ball with Joey and Katie in basement. Makes pork chops and creamed corn, and the best popcorn.

1976

Plays with friends in cemetery next to entrance to subdivision. Dark, quiet, forbidden, exciting. Feels gravestones, cold and smooth. Finds twenty-dollar bill on path. This is huge sum of money. Keeps it in room, on dresser, in small drawer of wooden decorative box. Keeps it there for years. Scared to even look at drawer—like piece of ghost-filled cemetery here in room—but equally hesitant to spend money.

1976

Laverne and Shirley *debuts. Amy is immediately troubled by* L *on Laverne's clothes. She asks her parents about it; can't fathom why this woman's sweaters and dresses have an* L. *Is told that* L *stands for Laverne (which Amy knew), that the monogrammed* L *is her trademark. Amy feels there has to be more to it than that. Someone had decided that Laverne would always wear an* L, *and this is not a usual thing from what Amy knows about the world so far. Amy is unable to watch* **Laverne and Shirley** *show without cursive* L *getting in the way.*

1976–1983

Amy wonders why the sign NO STANDEES *at front of the bus doesn't just say* NO STANDING.

1977

Amy does an aerial cartwheel for first time on lawn on side of her house. She finally succeeds by pretending there is someone spotting her.

1977

Amy rides her bike around subdivision with Anne and Rosalie, seems like hours. Talk about getting training bras. Feverish talk. Each girl relieved to hear other two have been thinking same thing.

1977

Uses Nair for the first time.

1977–1980

Junior high. Amy goes back-to-school shopping with her mother. She tries on clothes, then hands each item to her mother, who hangs it back on hanger, or reverses its inside-out status. Amy believes the new wool sweater, or plaid winter skirt, or corduroys and rugby shirt ensemble will make her look like Phoebe Cates in **Seventeen** *magazine. Amy not able to wait until it becomes cold out, and wears new fall outfits on third day of school. Is hot at recess. By afternoon, seventy-five degrees and sunny; she is very hot and itchy walking home.*

1977

Amy plays Billy Joel song "Movin' Out" over and over, trying to decipher and write down exact words. (He works at Mr. Caccitore's down on some other street . . . oh, wait, it's *Sullivan* Street.)

Wants to have one song that she will know all the words to, so when it comes on radio she will look cool nonchalantly singing along like Christy Buckin does.

1978

Eighth-grade student council elections. Classmate Cliff Norris hangs a huge banner. Amy thinks he is clever and sophisticated. However, message makes

her feel unsettled; cements what she has been sensing—unfamiliar terrain ahead, a place with new words and colors. Is scared.

Similarly, is confused and intimidated by band names like the Who, Dire Straits, Supertramp. Gets ones that are just names—James Taylor, Crosby, Stills & Nash. Non-name bands seem menacing in their incomprehensibility; stand for cooler, more sophisticated world not ready for.

1979

Amy begins dating Marc Richman at a bar mitzvah. Their anniversary is March 16. She loves Marc. Together off and on until freshman year of college.

1979

Gets her period, on the morning of her fourteenth birthday. Is in bedroom.

1980

Second semester freshman year, family moves to Lake Forest. Is livid. Does not talk to parents for a month. But gets good, private bedroom.

1980

With onset of puberty, weight emerges as new issue. In Florida for younger cousin's bar mitzvah, trying on skirt, hard to button, feels tight. Mother seems disapproving, frustrated. Amy feels hefty, especially compared to slim mother. Is instructed to wear panty hose with outfit—hates the way they cinch waist. Chubby more or less through teen years, with intermittent periods of grapefruit-induced weight loss. Jokes about wanting anorexia; thinks it would be nice in a way, but enjoys eating too much. Boy in high school calls her cute like Pillsbury Dough Boy; laughs it off but comment shakes her. Wonders if one day she will be thin enough that clavicle will jut out like mother's.

1980

Bread album really speaks to her.

1981

Sophomore year of high school. Amy shows up at school wearing a gold, twisty forehead band inspired by Olivia Newton-John's look from album **Physical**.

1981

While mother recovering from surgery in hospital, Amy tells father she's going to library to study; sneaks to boyfriend's house. As she's never been to library before, father suspicious, and drives to library to make sure car is there. Amy comes home to irate father. How could she be so deceitful, and selfish—for God's sake, mother in hospital. Regrets actions, is punished, is forgiven, but will be years before she fully comprehends scope of transgression.

1981

Gets violently sick on whiskey at friend's party. Never able to drink or smell it again.

1982

Amy loses her virginity.

—End of Childhood—

Clapping

Are there actually people who are so totally comfortable with themselves, so completely unself-conscious, that when they're at a concert and the band signals the audience to clap along, they can clap without thinking to themselves, *I am clapping now, here I am clapping along, are most people clapping? Okay, fine, most people are clapping, but wait, the clap-along thing feels like it's losing its momentum—should I stop clapping now? I'm feeling a bit heavy-handed in my clapping, but how/when do I stop? Three more claps and I'm out. Okay, last clap. Clap. Done.*

See also: Saturday Night Live

Closet

We were having a closet-organizing company redo a couple of our bedroom closets. On the morning they were supposed to do the work, we received a frantic call from the owner saying they had an unexpected closet emergency with another customer, and they'd have to reschedule. No problem, I said. For the life of me, though, I couldn't fathom what could possibly constitute a *closet emergency*.

Coffee, Stopping for

Waiting while our parents quick grabbed a to-go cup of coffee was not something we had to endure as kids—it did not exist. Stopping for coffee came onto the scene full force—via Starbucks—in the early 1990s, around the same time that I became a mother, so stopping for coffee is something my kids have grown up (and put up) with. Them as they see I'm pulling over and putting on hazards: *Oh, Mom.* Me: *Oh, Mom what. I'll just be a sec.* My guess is they, along with the rest of their generation, will ultimately connect stopping for coffee with their minivanesque childhoods.

I remember *per*fectly the first time I saw two cops with designer to-go cups in hand. They looked really silly. But that was the tipping point, when the whole thing graduated from trendy fad to way of life.

Then it became: My journey is enhanced if I have some coffee in the car cup holder, so how easy is it to incorporate a stop into my route, and do I have enough time to do so? Before getting on the highway: Yes, have to, no-brainer. On the way to a meeting: I'm already running late and parking sucks around there, hmmm . . . On the way to kids' chilly October soccer games: Definitely. One morning in July of '99 I stopped for a cup on the way to visit my grandma Mimi in the hospital. She died minutes before I arrived. That cup cost me.

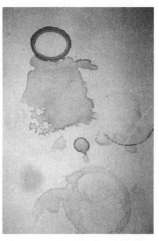

Coffee stain and random spill I noticed one morning in my office. I thought it looked like an angel.

The same way that movies set in the 1800s show gents casually tying up their horses to wooden posts—and doesn't it immediately place you in that time, and make you think about horses versus cars?—future filmmakers doing an early-twenty-first-century period piece should definitely include stopping-for-coffee scenes. Props department: Make sure the cups have cardboard jackets and collapsed bowler hat sipping lids.

Then there's the cream-and-sugar-station tango, which we're now all adept at. You get to the bar. You twirl the oversized Thermoses around, in search of the whole milk, perhaps. Guy comes up who needs 2 percent Thermos next to you; you sway your upper body and neck back as if to say, *Go ahead, I don't need it, all yours.* You take an Equal packet, pinch the top and flick it a couple times, so the powder all settles or something—don't know, it's just habit—then tear it open, pour. And now, the last step, snag a stirrer. Lift your arm up . . . and over the fellow, higher than is necessary so as to respect his space, not step on toes. Exit and out.

COFFEEHOUSE

My coffeehouse died. The one I went to every single Thursday for three years, minus a couple sore throats, vacations, and childbirths. The one where I wrote or tried to write or thought about trying to write. The one where I ate ham-and-cheese sandwiches, tofu asiago melts, and bagels with basil cream cheese. The one where I would sit for hours and sip and sip (never enough water). It was called Urbus Orbis, and I loved it.

I fancied Chicago's Urbus as the kind of coffeehouse/salon you would have once found in Paris's 4th Arrondissement. I'm totally making this up; I should know more about the history and role of European coffeehouses, but I'm rather attached to the smoky notions I've adopted as fact: Passion. Pretension. Unnecessary gesticulating. Cigarettes that didn't cause cancer. And pencils that caused revolutions.

Urbus's decor was Late-Twentieth-Century Thrown Together, which I think for a coffeehouse is a good thing. Like your college English prof, Urbus was brimming with personality and papers that needed shuffling. There was that wonderful William Carlos Williams poem about the plums painted up the stairs. And graffiti was the legacy of every smart-ass who ever graced Urbus's bathroom.

We saw it coming. The once messy, artsy Wicker Park neighborhood where it held court is now the Midwest's answer to

Soho and South Beach—not that any of us ever asked the question. The rent at Urbus eventually became higher than the heavily caffeinated clientele.

I'm still in a mourning period now, drinking my coffee black. I keep calling up the owner, Tom—who I guess is the Ponytailed Widow in this dramedy—staying connected to the past under the guise of checking up on him post-Urbus/pre—whatever's next. I ran into another regular last week and our giddy enthusiasm had nothing to do with liking each other, and everything to do with liking Urbus.

Growing up in a family of four children and a TV, I quickly learned not so much how to tune out chaos, as how to ride its energy as I memorized spelling words, practiced my multiplication tables, and skimmed *The Hobbit*. The point is, I liked writing at Urbus precisely because it was chaotic and garlicky and alive. I've been reading about different writers' colonies lately, and apparently these cubicles in the woods seem to just breed Pulitzer Prize winners, but I suspect that for me, all the . . . *nothing* would do just that for my work.

As Urbus became synonymous with Thursday, Thursday became synonymous with Charise. We met on a blind date of sorts—a mutual friend noticed we had similar interests and shoes. Charise and I would spend the afternoon basically just cheering each other on. *Oh, Charise—that illustration is amazing! Thanks, Amy, and I love that sentence you just wrote!* Intermittently, we would invent projects and experiments to collaborate on, as a way of justifying our sixth cup of coffee—the last venture being a lemonade stand where, for a quarter, the customer could buy a glass of lemonade, an

Thursday—painting by Charise Mericle Harper.

illustration of lemonade, or a paragraph about lemonade. More often than not, though, we were just happy to share rejection letters, a table, and the cream.

I want to say that I miss Urbus. I miss the slow service, and the way they never remembered the tomato that I ordered with my bagel. I miss the chalkboard menu that tended to be inaccurate. I miss the bathroom sink that only ran scalding-hot water. I miss the matchbooks under the table legs. I miss Tom's house special: the tasty illusion of mattering.

And I want to say, *Excuse me, but I thought I ordered a bottomless cup.*

COMFORT IN THE EXPECTED

Comfort in the expected manifests itself in less overt ways, too. Like let's say you have a mixed tape (now we make compilation CDs; back in the day, it was mixed tapes), and you come to know not just the order of the songs but the exact pausing in between, and then when you happen to hear one of those songs on their original album, it really throws you.

See also: Improvisation at Concerts

COMMENCEMENT ADDRESS

Mark all your college photos now, with names and dates. You think you'll never forget these people, but you will; the last name of one of my college beaus escaped me for three entire years. It is now time to give the milk crates to a freshman and get yourself some real bookshelves. From this point on, you will be required to correctly use *it's* and *its.* This would be the year to backpack through Europe, date all the wrong people, and temp at a sushi bar. Now is the time to take up guitar and work on your cursive *M*'s. Your first job will most likely be in an office of some kind. When you jam the Xerox machine, lift the side door and follow the simple instructions. Or walk away and return an hour later—surely someone will have fixed it by then. Chances are, you will either hate your boss or fall in love with him/her. Both are normal, if not inevitable. Regarding these phrases:

> *Let's try to push the envelope.*
> *Think outside the box.*
> *I've got a lot on my plate.*
> *I want to make sure we're on the same page.*
> *Things are really crazy this week.*

Many people before you have said these things many times; they sounded foolish each time. There is no need for you to resort to this office-speak, ever. Take every single one of your vacation days.

Have children, if you're so inclined, but before you breed, sleep a lot. And when you order takeout, make sure to check the bag before you leave the restaurant.

COMPLETION

I eat quickly, purposefully, and almost always finish everything on my plate. I finish the meal so I can get to dessert. I finish the dessert so I can get up from the table. When I'm out, I'm usually thinking about going home. When I'm home, I'm usually thinking about the next time I'm going out. I find deleting e-mails or messages on my answering machine quite gratifying. I have not experienced the full pleasure of an act or task until I've crossed it off my list. I'm thrilled when leftovers finally become stale so I can throw them out. Wednesdays are special—it's when the garbagemen come. I like it when we finish one of our half-gallons of milk, so I can rinse it out and put the glass bottle out back for the milkman. I tend to see movies right when they come out because it bothers me to know it's something I still have to do. I always hated Monopoly—the end was invariably nowhere in sight. Magazines full of too many good articles make me frantic. I fantasize about getting rid of everything in my closet except for an outfit or two. I love mailing letters—specifically, letting them drop out of my hand into the mailbox's metal cavern. I find myself throwing away, say, a jar of peanut butter or bottle of shampoo when there's still a small amount left because the satisfaction of disposing of it far outweighs the option of keeping it in my life for some future spoonful or drop. An emptied dishwasher is a pleasing sight. My favorite command on the computer is *Empty Trash*. When I'm driving, my mind is fixed on the destination. My all-time favorite play is *Too Much Light Makes the Baby Go Blind*, which consists of thirty very short plays performed within sixty minutes, under the constraints of an egg timer placed onstage. I enjoy cooking because recipes offer a very manageable list of instructions to continuously complete, not to mention the joy I get from using up the ingredients. The concept of infinity makes me nuts.

See also: Magazines

COMPLIMENT

While getting my annual checkup at the doctor's, the nurse says, as she's preparing to draw blood from my arm, *You've got great veins. Thanks,* I say, as if it were a compliment, as if I had anything to do with the creation of my veins. If someone says, *You've got a great backhand,* that's something you can actually take credit for; your backhand may have sucked before, but after many tennis lessons and months of practice, you were able to improve it. Fine. Your ego is then entitled to process *you've got a great backhand* as a compliment. But under no circumstances can *you've got great veins* be taken as a legitimate compliment.

CONNECTED (VERSUS REMOVED)

When I read a magazine, I feel connected to the world, in on everything. When I read a book, I feel removed from the world, isolated, as if I've slipped off into a soundproof booth. It is the same with listening to the radio (connected) versus listening to a CD (removed). Both fill a certain need, balance the other out. There's the getting away, and then there's the coming back.

CONVERSATION

Standing in a doorway and chatting is safe; one has, literally and figuratively, an easy out. But the slightest gesture—taking a step in, glancing at a chair in the corner, unraveling a scarf—signals a commitment to a full-blown conversation. Similarly, if one is interrupted while reading a book, a thumb in the book signals an allegiance to the book, and the interrupter should expect only the most cursory reply. But if the book gets shut with a bookmark, or placed down open-faced, a full conversation will most likely follow.

COOL

I didn't realize just how far away I was from being cool, successful, and taut until I read about a breed of attractive, young, hip multimillionaires in halter tops throwing all-night raves in Silicon Valley.

CREAM RINSE

Cream rinse always gets stuck in the upper rim of my right ear. Not my left ear. And never shampoo. Just the right ear, cream rinse. I will be driving and glance at myself in the rearview mirror and spot white goo hanging out in there. I'm always like, *Again! The cream rinse! What's up with this?!* as I wipe it off. You'd think I'd make a special mental note to do some focused right- ear rinsing in the shower, but I never think about it until later, usually when I'm in a public place. Amazingly, no one has ever said anything to me about the white glob in my upper ear. Whether this is because it's usually sufficiently hidden by my hair or because it's too awkward for someone to bring up, I don't know. *So nice to meet you. I'm glad we'll be working together. Uh . . . you have . . . uh . . .*

CREAM SAUCE

I love any kind of cream sauce. My mother hates cream sauce but craved it when she was pregnant with me.

See also: Meaning

CROSSING GUARD

I was walking down Lincoln Avenue when I overheard a crossing guard say to some older gentleman hanging out on the corner, *Yeah, work's been crazy around here—I've been really busy.* I tried to picture the circumstances that would account for this statement. Perhaps when it's a nice sunny day, crossing guards wake up and say, *Dang! Everyone's gonna be out walking today—work is going to be insane.*

See also: Busy

CROUTONS

Unusual and delicious croutons can be made simply by using corn bread in place of French or sourdough. I simply get the pre-made corn bread (available in most bakery sections), cut it up into little chunks, toss with some olive oil, and bake in a 350-degree oven until golden brown, about twenty minutes or so.

CURLY HAIR

Curly hair is more original.

CUSTOMARY, THINGS THAT ARE

Table
Companies specializing in paying people to lose thirty pounds customarily advertise via crappy, hand-scrawled signs—WE'LL PAY YOU TO LOSE WEIGHT!—tacked to street poles.
A hearty bread customarily has nine grains.
Couples customarily take a cruise on their ten-year anniversary.
It is customary to serve buffalo wings, but no other kind of chicken, with blue cheese dressing.
It is customary to de-blandize the walls of one's office cubicle by tacking up Internet-circulated anecdotes and jokes, inspirational quotes, and personal photos of babies/pets/ski trips, all intended to subtly reveal one's true, interesting self, but which only a handful of months later will seem embarrassing in their earnestness, simplicity, and triteness.
When people go up to a microphone, they customarily say, "Check—one, two, check."
(continued)

Fractures are customarily one millimeter away from something much more serious. "The doctor said that if the fracture had been one millimeter to the left, I'd be dead." Growths, for their part, are customarily compared to the size of fruits: a grape, an orange, a grapefruit.

When the waiter comes to take your order, it is customary to open your menu and glance at it even though you already know what you're having.

Airplane magazines customarily have ads for companies that will put your logo on a watch.

D

DEEP MASSAGE

If I'm getting a massage and the massage therapist happens to be applying too much pressure, I find it nearly impossible to tell her that it's too hard, even if I'm in a great deal of pain. What, like this would really devastate her in some way? In all other non-massage life situations, I have no problem being bold, even at the risk of being overbearing. But for some reason, lying there, being slowly bruised, I can't seem to speak up, and I will formulate in my mind all the ways I might broach the subject for the duration of the massage.

DELI TRAYS

Tragedy-oriented and celebration-oriented gatherings both seem to result in deli trays.

I've got twenty people coming for a holiday party—can I get your deli meat platter?

I've got a hundred people coming here after a funeral—I'll take two pounds of salami, one pound of . . .

DENTIST

I went to the dentist for an annual cleaning. I had started flossing regularly and was looking forward to the inevitable moment of recognition: *Wow, Amy, great job flossing.* I kept waiting, but it was as if he didn't notice. I brought it up as tactfully as possible—*So, Doc, can you tell I took your advice about flossing more?*—but of course that wasn't nearly as rewarding.

Depressing, Things That I Find

Table

Flipping through an issue of *Cat Magazine* at doctor's office. Sections had titles like "What's Mew" and "Purrsonals."

Logo for a local hair salon, something about the turquoise swish.

Male model getting his hair cut next to Miles at Supercuts. Couldn't help but overhear him telling the stylist about his glamorous jaunts to Germany for big photo shoot, all-expense-paid this, limo that. The desperation inherent in bragging about himself and his imagined fabulousness to this very sweet, very polite woman who, let's face it, didn't understand English very well, was disturbing.

At toy store, the kids had to go to the bathroom, so they let us go in back to employee restroom. Spotted a sign from manager reminding employees to BE PROFOSSIONAL!

Abrupt receptionists who transfer me without any verbal niceties or warning.

Restaurants that put quotes around words that do not require quotes. Usually on window signage. For example: Freddy's Authentic "Greek Food."

Former *Seinfeld* actor Jason Alexander doing Kentucky Fried Chicken commercial.

Newsletters from school that are chirpy and congratulatory: "We raised $4,000 at last month's Bowl 'n' Bake Sale—great job everyone!!!"

Page 147 of a book titled *Mastery*. The word *it's* is misused.

Dessert

My kids keep asking me at dessert time, *Mom, can I have this little pack of Skittles and this piece of gum?* or (looking through their Halloween loot) *How about this mini Baby Ruth and a candy cane?* I take a quick look at the items they are holding up in their hands and, without hesitation, assess the inventory and respond accordingly. *You can have half the candy cane and the mini Baby Ruth.* They accept my arbitrary ruling as gospel, as if it stems from some great unwavering truth.

Dialogue

Charise (blonde): *How would I look with red hair?*
Doug (husband): *Lonely.*

Directions

When someone gives you directions to their house, there is always a point where you realize, *I think they are giving me way more detail than necessary.* People think they are helping you by saying *You'll turn left at the first light. There'll be an Arby's on the right and a little church with white shutters and this funny dolphin sculpture on the left. If you see a Blockbuster—and I think there's a Hooters there, too—then you've gone too far.* We could all be a little more sparing with the landmark usage.

Director's Commentary

I originally thought the DVD Director's Commentary feature was a cool idea, an enriching bonus for the viewer. But after listening to a handful of them, I've come to realize that they are really nothing more than a love-fest opportunity for the two commentators. Take *The Contender,* for example. I am way into that movie, and couldn't wait to hear what the director and Joan Allen had to say. But then, this:

Director: Remember we first met at that one award banquet? I knew then that I just had to write a movie for you.

Joan: I get a lot of scripts and have developed a healthy skepticism, but wow, your script really stood out.

Director: Jeff [Bridges] wouldn't sign on until you were officially on board.

Joan: I just love Jeff's work. I think he is simply brilliant.

I'm all for mutual admiration, and I agree that Jeff Bridges is brilliant, but this type of banter is really not for public consumption.

Dishwasher

It is very difficult to try to load someone else's dishwasher; everyone has their own method. Glasses stacked in this row, bowls this way, silverware facing up, down—it's a highly personal thing. The few times someone outside the family has loaded ours, I open it up and am disoriented, dismayed even, to find plates in the wrong slots, bowls on the top (the top?!), and even a skillet crammed in there. It's just too counterproductive and unsettling, even though it is nice of them to try to help.

Distraction

I recognize that everything I do, from my work to going to the movies to raising children to vacuuming, might also be viewed as just one big distraction—*Hey, look over here! And now, over here!*—from belaboring the real issue at hand: One day I'm going to die.

Doctor in the House

At Rosh Hoshana services, a man scurried up and down the aisles asking, "Is there a doctor in the house? We need a doctor. Is there a doctor?" There was much scuttling about, heads turning this way and that, what happened, who's hurt. When I saw a woman dash to the exit, it took a moment for it to register that the doctor had been located, that she, this woman, was the doctor. Despite my supposedly liberal and feminist leanings, I'd imagined a man—older, with S.O.S-pad eyebrows—emerging heroically from the crowd.

See also: Feminist

Doing Something

It is so much easier to not do something than to do something. Even the smallest task, like filling out a Scholastic Books order form or putting away the butter, requires time, focus, and follow-through. It's astounding, actually, that anything gets done at all, by anyone.

But then, let's say you finally are prepared and determined to do that thing, whatever it is, but you wake up to find that your basement has flooded and you must spend your day making phone calls to the contractor, plumber, and carpet people. Or not that but something else—perhaps you must stand before a committee for approval, a committee that neither grasps your intent nor appreciates your ingenuity, and anyway, they are in a bit of a hurry to break for lunch.

Yet. Still. Somehow. I am encouraged to see that despite the colossal effort, despite the odds against one, despite the mere constraints of time and schedules and sore throats, houses do get built, pottery gets glazed, e-mails get sent, trees get planted, shoes get reheeled, manifestos get Xeroxed, films get shot, highways get repaved, cakes get frosted, stories get told.

DOOR

At the restaurant, we were seated by the door. Throughout the course of our meal, we observed dozens of patrons do the following, in this exact order:

Walk up to the door and try pulling it.

Confused, they would try pulling it again, only to confirm that it was indeed locked.

Then they'd cup their hands around their eyes, put their faces up to the glass, peek inside and see people sitting down, eating, and then be more confused.

Finally, they'd notice the sign taped to the door:

**PLEASE ENTER
THROUGH BAR
TONIGHT**

Simultaneously relieved and annoyed, they'd walk toward the other door.

It was intriguing and comforting to watch this, something about the rhythm and the predictability of it, the succession, one after the other, of happy endings.

DOORBELL

The doorbell rings. You are either expecting someone or you are not. If you are expecting someone, you think, *Yes, okay, they are here.* If you are not expecting someone, you think, *That's curious. I am not expecting anyone—who could it be?* Now, if the phone rings, whether you are expecting a call or not, you think, *Oh, the phone is ringing, someone is calling me.* With the phone, you know it is just as likely that it could be a person you are expecting to call or any other number of people you are not expecting, or even know.

DRAWING

I can't really draw. As a kid, though, I drew all the time; by middle school, even though I wasn't all that good, I became known as *the artist.* Markers and paints and ink pens were what I knew, what was readily available. It would still be awhile until I discovered how words and writing could be used as a possible creative outlet.

If I could draw, I would have been able to figure out how to make a woman with long hair pulled back look different from a woman with short hair. If I could draw, I wouldn't stop at the face, I would enjoy adding arms as well. If I could draw, I would have a lot of excellent art supplies in my house. And I would probably sketch people and then give it to them as a present.

See also: Toast

DREAMS

I am an avid dreamer. I have multiple epic dreams nearly every night. When this fact comes up, I usually work *Yeah, I always say I should go to sleep with a bowl of popcorn* into the conversation. I rarely share my dreams because I believe dreams are only fascinating to the person who had them. The exception to that is if you are in someone else's dream—then of course you want to hear about it. My old journals are full of dream descriptions. Though this contradicts the sentence before last, here is one uncharacteristically brief entry from March 2, 1984: *I was in this dark little room and I started dancing real seductively up against the wall. Then I did a front walkover across the floor.* Inconsequential, I know, but I do like that on that day exactly seven years later, I married Jason.

See also: Husband; Jason

From: TheGood515@aol.com

Date: Thu, 10 Apr 2003 13:02:20 EDT

Subject: Dream

To: missamykr@yahoo.com

Amy,

I think you mentioned that other people's dreams aren't interesting unless
you're in them. I agree. But I just remembered having a dream last night that
I was performing my show at night at Schubas, and you were performing/orchestrating some big revue that would begin after my show. It
was a packed house, bench-style seating like you see in movies about old-time, small-town theatrical events. We were supposed to start at 10:30,
but you kept fussing with the stage, which was behind curtains, and I had to
do my show with all of your props in waiting. All I remember is a big chair
with lots of different outfits on it. I started absentmindedly moving them
aside and you said, "no no, those have to stay there." Things were running
late already when we finally had our chance to start getting ready. Michael,
my director, was so busy schmoozing with the crowd he could not help me at
all (not a stretch), and I seemed to have misplaced all of my props and
devices. It was literally a nightmare. At one point I realized it was 11:30
and we had not even begun the show. I couldn't imagine what time you would
start your show. Oh, and lots of people had brought small children. That's
it, I don't remember any more. You decide the significance.

Tony

Tony's Dream

Dry Cleaners

Today when I was picking up my dry cleaning, the owner said, "Wait, before you go, this envelope—we found ten dollars in your pocket last week." It was a white envelope, with these words in blue pen: "Rosenthal, $10, from the pocket on shirt, March 6, 2000."

Such a gesture, putting aside this found money, money he could have so easily taken—we would have never known. The sealed envelope sealed the money's fate. So honest and kind. He wrote our name on it to be sure to give it to us. *Rosenthal. From the pocket on shirt.*

See also: Rosendal

Drying Off

When I get out of the shower, I never dry off properly—that is to say, slowly and thoroughly dry my entire body, limb by limb, torso, back. I simply wrap the towel around myself, and then, feeling dry enough, start getting dressed. My old boyfriend used to comment on this: *Why don't you ever dry off?* My husband occasionally comments on me dripping from the bedroom to our closet. I don't think that I'm in a rush exactly, because I often take very long showers. It's more that when the shower is over, I seem to just want to proceed directly to the next phase: being dressed. I am accustomed to feeling a light dampness, particularly on my legs under my jeans, the first couple minutes I'm dressed.

Dying

There are so many ways to die at any given moment. Just look, look at all those ambulances in your rearview mirror. There are crashes and wrecks and collisions galore: cars, planes, Amtraks, ferries. You could have a heart attack; it's not unlikely. A terminal illness you didn't even know you had could, minutes from now, live up to its defining adjective. Now turn your attention to all the freak accidents lurking in the wings. A massive store display tips over (happened). A soccer goal post unroots itself and crushes a skull (happened). Shelving holding five thousand pounds of sheet metal or lumber at Home Depot collapses (imagined). A top bunk falls onto the bottom bunk (imagined). A strong wind unhinges scaffolding and blows it directly onto a sports car; inside are—were—two twenty-year-olds out shopping (happened). Aneurisms that burst midsentence, ending the life of an advertising executive, a promising playwright, a children's book author (happened, happened, and happened). I think almost weekly about an article I read years and years ago in *Reader's Digest*: A mother and daughter were driving along when an overhead highway sign fell, instantly killing the girl and removing her face. The timing of that—the position of the car, how fast they were driving, where and when the sign landed—was horrifyingly impeccable. And this: A young couple killed in a car accident on the way to her father's funeral. Have you ever? And I'm not even touching on the human-calculated varieties: shooting, stabbing, strangulation by (a) someone you know, (b) someone you don't know, (c) someone disgruntled (postal worker, unappreciated employee, failing student). And we can't forget malpractice. My sister-in-law died at the age of thirty-two during childbirth because the doctors and nurses missed the red-flagged *allergic to anesthesia* warning on her medical chart. People don't die anymore in childbirth, everyone knows that, but yet they do; sweet, stunning, silk-scarf-wearing, multilingual Hilary did. People are just dying everywhere, all the time, every which way. What can the rest of us do but hold on for dear life.

E

The French writer Georges Perec is most famous for writing a three-hundred-page novel without using a single *e*. One can envision the everyday small talk that must have occurred while Mr. Perec was working on this book.

> *Bonjour, Georges.*
> *Bonjour, Pascal.*
> *What are you working on these days?*
> *I'm trying to write an entire novel without using the letter* e.
> Silence
> *Did I tell you, Georges, about our new porch?*

Egg-White Scrambler

I went out for brunch with my dad. I ordered the breakfast burrito. It turned out to be way too much: too many eggs, too much cheese. A few bites into it, a waitress waltzes over to the table next to ours with two orders of this happy light plate of scrambled egg whites and diced tomato and a touch of cheese. Their waitress had obviously let them in on this special-order item. It was the dream version of my dish. The women were oohing as she placed it before them. *Yeah, it's my favorite,* the waitress cooed with them, only adding to my misery.

The ridiculous thing is, I couldn't get it out of my head for the rest of the afternoon. I'd be driving or washing my hands or looking up a word in the thesaurus, and my mind would keep going back to the egg-white scrambler. I imagined how it would taste, thought about when I'd go back to that restaurant, imagined how my day, my entire life, would have been so much better if only I'd had that egg-white scrambler.

EITHER

It's either *I don't like you. You are just like me. Your presence confirms much of what I don't like about myself* or *I like you. You are just like me. Your presence confirms much of what I like about myself.*

ENCOURAGEMENT, EXERCISE VIDEO INSTRUCTOR WHO TRIES TO GIVE

When the instructor on an exercise video says *great!* and *good job!* and *yes, that's it!*, it's so patronizing. She can't see me; how can she possibly comment on my performance? Are we humans that pathetic and praise-thirsty that an instructor spewing generic affirmations to an invisible audience is considered helpful, effective, and believable? I put on one such tape and felt not encouraged but rather enraged by the unfounded compliments. When her fifth *yes, there you go!* elicited an under-my-breath *shut the fuck up*, I knew it was time to turn off the tape.

ENCYCLOPEDIA SPINE

I was talking with my friend Marie-Claude shortly after finishing the first draft of this book. She said, *Speaking of encyclopedias, I have to tell you this unreal but true story. You know my friend ——, right? Well, she used to work at Encyclopedia Britannica. She was working on a new edition. And I've actually seen this at the library, so I promise you I'm not making this up: On the spine of volume eight, it says Menage—Ottawa. That was her doing. The editors apparently never picked up on it.* I ran to the library to see for myself.

Entrance Sign

There's always the option to process it not as the intended noun (point of entry) but rather as the verb, to fascinate.

Escalator

One would think that by this point in my life, I would have outgrown the fear of getting my shoe caught in the escalator.

See also: Anxious, Things That Make Me; Fears

Euphoric

The child is euphoric because there is an elevator button that needs pressing. Or perhaps a moon is spotted in a daytime sky.

F

FAME

When someone becomes hugely famous and they go home for the regular Thanksgiving and Passover family gatherings, it must be weird for everyone else, pulling into the driveway of your aunt Barbara and uncle Henry knowing that your cousin Cameron (*Cammy* to you) Diaz will be there.

FAMOUS, HOW YOU KNOW YOU ARE

Table
You have a level of a parking garage named after you, with accompanying sound track. "Remember where you are parked: You are on Level 4 Barbra Streisand: The early years."
An article written about you in a magazine or newspaper has a photo of you from your high-school yearbook, so the world can see what you looked like with feathered hair, pre-fame.
Kraft Macaroni and Cheese comes out with a special noodle shaped in your likeness. Note: This is usually reserved for cartoon celebrities, such as the Rugrats, Pokémon, or Blue's Clues.
You get stopped on the street, not because you are famous, but because you look familiar. "I'm sorry, but did I go to school with you? I know I know you. Wait, were you at Lindy's fortieth last weekend? Oh my God"—*click*—"I'm so sorry, you're Neve Campbell. I knew you looked familiar."

FARMER

There is a sentence in a book called *Paris to the Moon* that goes something like this:

We had a framer who regularly did all of our framing for us. But when I first read the sentence I thought the author wrote, *We had a FARMER who regularly did all of our framing for us.* In the flash of 1.5 seconds my mind processed this misinformation and produced, rather clearly, the image of a farmer (somewhere in rural Vermont?) who, either in need of supplemental income or just out of a love for framing, developed a little frame business out of his farm, attracting a small but loyal customer base from nearby towns and even New York (where the author was living, I know). It wasn't exactly the typical kind of frame business I'm accustomed to, but somehow, for that split second, I was intrigued by and accepting of this farmer-framer situation. I could picture his wife coming into his barn/work space. *Another great frame, honey! You've been working so hard, I brought you a glass of lemonade.* When I reread and correctly comprehended the sentence, I was instantly sad to let go of the eccentric character I had come to know, to find that the framer was just like any framer—that is to say, nondescript, cynical, urban, working part-time at a shop with overpriced frames and Henri Cartier-Bresson posters on the wall.

See also: Cheek Bouncing; Words That Look Similar

FEARS

I am scared of the dark, and of our garage, basement, and any mirrors at night.

FEEL LIKE MYSELF

I make my sevens with a cross through the middle, same with my Z's—when I try to write them without crossing, it feels uncomfortably unfinished and I have the urge to make the cross. I have been wearing the same perfume, Fracas, since eighth grade, when my boyfriend Marc's mother introduced it to me. When I run into people I haven't seen for a long time, they will invariably remark, *You smell the same, you smell like Amy.* I wear mascara and eyeliner, but I never ever wear rouge, no matter how pale I am; I must have a teen memory of feeling makeup-y and clownlike with it brushed along my freckled cheekbones. I took my watch off when I was twenty-three and haven't worn one since. I have had long hair most of my life; I'll occasionally get bored and cut it, then start to not feel like myself and grow it back. If I don't like the shoes I have on, I feel plain, even if I like the rest of my outfit. I hate wearing socks, and resort to them only in extreme weather conditions. I simply do not like the way they feel on my feet. Friends often comment, *it is freezing out, and you're not wearing any socks!* I look down, *I know, I know,* I say. Or they e-mail me about some dinner plans and say, *P.S. Put on some socks!* I have not worn panty hose since I left for college, no matter how dressy the occasion; they feel like the leg equivalent of foundation makeup: false, itchy, and not me. I like my toenails painted, and my fingernails short and unpainted. I do not feel like myself in nice jewelry— I wear a two-dollar thumb ring and a five-dollar toe ring. I stopped wearing earrings altogether in my late twenties. I gravitate toward thrift-shop jackets. I am not a purse person. Maybe it has to do with being small; I feel like a girl playing dress-up, like what am I doing with this fancy thing. I bought a brown leather backpack in Greece when I was twenty-four and have been carrying it around ever since. It is now very worn-in, and feels very much like me.

[Offering]
Fracas was created in 1948 by Robert Piguet.
It blends jasmine, gardenia, lily of the valley, and white iris.
A complimentary sample is available
to the first one hundred readers to request it.
(encyclopediaofanordinarylife.com)

FEMINIST

Can you be a feminist yet still do a double take when you see a woman UPS driver?

See also: Doctor in the House

FICTION

I am not attracted to fiction, and I feel bad about this; I perceive it is a weakness, but what can you do. I can't read fiction without wondering, *Is this part true? Is that part about the grizzly attack true? If it didn't happen to the author, who did it happen to, and are they okay?* The other thing with fiction is that the inevitable paragraphs about the weather/sky/trees instantly derail me.

> *There was a gentle breeze. There was a gust of wind. It was cold. It was hot. There were birds, a still lake, a pond, an ocean, mountains, birds chirping, city sounds, tall trees, bare trees, trees casting shadows, a blue sky, a black sky, a sunset sky, a round white moon.*

On with it. So what about the moon? There it is, it's very cool, I love the moon, too, we all like the moon, the moon is fascinating, what with space travel and men bouncing in those fat suits up there. But what do all the moon adjectives (full, half, a sliver) have to do with Josie (the redheaded, diabetic protagonist) shopping for lawn furniture with her ex-husband? Other people appreciate these descriptions, and I'm trying to be like them; I want to be like them. Please help me. Show me a story that describes a moon in a new way, in a way that matters, in a way that will make everything okay. If you could e-mail me that passage, I'd be most grateful.

Fifteen Minutes

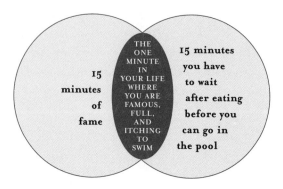

15 minutes of fame

THE ONE MINUTE IN YOUR LIFE WHERE YOU ARE FAMOUS, FULL, AND ITCHING TO SWIM

15 minutes you have to wait after eating before you can go in the pool

Fifty States

I can rattle off the fifty states in alphabetical order in seventeen seconds.

Flahoolick

Flahoolick is an Irish word meaning openhanded, generous, expansive, and oh much else. . . . Anything can be flahoolick under certain conditions. Even water, supposing you were crawling on your hands and knees across the desert and in the broiling sun and came upon a waterfall though what it would be doing there we are not prepared to say. Lemon squash can be flahoolick if you are nine years old or inordinately fond of lemon squash. Draught beer is flahoolick; large linen napkins are flahoolick; long nightshirts are virtually always flahoolick.
   —Howard Gossage, advertising writer, 1917—1969

It's such a great word—in and of itself flahoolick. It feels good to say: You've got the *fla* action and the *hoo,* and then the satisfying crispness of the final syllable, a syllable that happens to be a word that conjures up lollipops.

In the course of our daily generic routine, we seem programmed to seek out that which is flahoolick, to arm ourselves with flahoolick antibodies. Stopping for a cup of coffee on our way to work is an instant jolt of flahoolickness—and it goes beyond the caffeine; the tingle begins in the ordering of the coffee, the anticipation of the treat, the receiving, the way you feel walking out with the hot cardboard (crutch) in your hand. When my mother-in-law plays bridge online and the deep, anonymous voice says, "Nice move," it makes her happy, or at least makes her momentarily immune to nonhappiness, because it is flahoolick. Similarly, my neighbor trained her parrot to say, "Hi, Cutie!" every time she enters the room. She may think she did this because it is novel and amusing, but on some level she did this because it is flahoolick to be greeted by someone who is clearly glad to see you.

Soft pita bread dipped in Baba Ganoush is flahoolick.

Hearing NPR correspondent Sylvia Poggioli say her name is flahoolick. SIL-vi-A Pa-JO-li.

A lit-up Ferris wheel in the distance is flahoolick.

FLIGHT HABITS

I always start off clean and organized when I fly. I tuck my magazines and earphones in the seat pocket, place my backpack neatly under the seat in front of me, lay my book on my lap . . . but about twenty minutes after takeoff, I've got papers everywhere, pens have fallen between the cushion crevices, pretzel and earphone wrappers are strewn on the floor, and one of my shoes has disappeared way under the seat.

FLYING

When the captain announces we're beginning our descent, and we're still pretty high above the city, I'll think, *If the plane went down now, we would definitely not be okay. A bit lower, and no, we still wouldn't be okay. Maybe now, now we might be low enough that if it crashed, we might be okay.*

FOLDED QUILTS

Marie-Claude bought a beautiful antique cabinet with glass doors, repainted it, and filled it with a small stack of nicely folded handmade quilts. It is a joy to look at. It doesn't mean to, but it represents everything my life currently is not. It's fair to say I covet the cabinet. I hope to one day have the time and wherewithal to dote on such a fine item.

FOLDING CHAIRS

I called a rental company to see about renting some folding chairs. An older gentleman answered. He sounded jovial, full-bellied, possibly wearing suspenders. As he asked me questions—*how many chairs? what day do you need them?*—I could hear a woman in the background. It became clear that they were business partners, and that they were husband and wife. Every time he asked me something, she would correct him, or say, *Did you ask her _____ ?* just before he was about to ask me that. I could picture her—small, in a tent dress—standing about four feet diagonally behind him.

FREE TO BE . . . YOU AND ME

I was talking with a friend about how much we loved the *Free to Be . . . You and Me* album when we were kids. The theme song.

The two newborns, played by Mel Brooks and Marlo Thomas. "William's Doll." "It's All Right to Cry." "Dudley Pippin and the Principal." I listen to it now, with my kids, and it's bittersweet. Its production style exudes 1972, something about the piano and the background chorus and the tinniness. It's how Saturday-morning cartoon theme songs sounded. It's how movie theme songs sounded. It's how that whole decade sounded.

My friend was saying she hadn't heard the album in years, and I told her I had an extra copy I could give her; it was a bit scratched, but she could have it. In fact, I could bring it to her the next night because we had just figured out that, just by chance, we had dinner reservations at the same restaurant.

On the way to the restaurant I listened to the two CDs to figure out which was the scratched one. I realize a bigger person would keep the scratched one and pass on the clean copy. When my husband and I pulled up in front of the restaurant, *Free to Be* was blasting through our speakers.

When we returned to our car a few hours later, after having successfully passed off the scratched CD to our friend, the valet guy hops out of the driver's seat and says, *Dude! That was awesome! I'm not kidding you, I haven't heard* Free to Be . . . You and Me *since I was a kid!*

FRENCH FRIES

How great is it to find a few stray bonus fries at the bottom of your McDonald's bag?

See also: Q-Tip

FRIEND YOU THOUGHT CONFIDED IN YOU

You think the friend is confiding in you, and in you alone. See, he is telling you something important here; he's sharing personal details, and excerpts from a confrontational dialogue between him and X. He has chosen to share this with you because you are a rare kind of friend, and he values your opinion and unique brand of feedback. Yep, you're good friends, the two of you. But a few sentences into his saga, something in his story triggers him to say, *Did I already tell you this?* And that, bam, is the instant giveaway. He has told others, most likely many others—hell, he can't even keep track. No, you were not handpicked at all. He just wants to talk about this, over and over, doesn't really matter with whom. You were simply the next one up. Now you don't even want to hear the rest of the story, let alone give him advice; who cares about his dumb personal life.

See also: Humbling; Running into Someone; Special

G

GAS TANK

Every. Single. Solitary. Time I go to get gas I have to lean out the window to see which side the tank is on.

GLOVE

I dropped my glove. As soon as I realized it, I turned around and retraced my steps. I couldn't find it anywhere. I couldn't imagine where it could be. Would I be able to find it if, say, my life depended on me finding it? I mean, literally, if someone said, *Find that glove or we will kill you,* would I be able to find it? I imagined spending hour after hour searching for it, in bushes, under cars. I would have to interview people who were on the street at the time. I would have to get everyone's phone number right now, every single person on the street. And then, because so many people are already gone, I'd have to put flyers up on street poles and trees. *Were you on this street at 8:45 A.M. Friday? Have you seen this glove?*

I would talk to many people about the glove. Someone would recall seeing it in a puddle. No, finding this glove would not be easy.

GLUE

I asked Jason to pick up some glue traps at the hardware store. He didn't read the list I had given him closely, so he came home not with glue traps but just glue—in fact, two kinds, Elmer's and super glue. As I was emptying the plastic bag, I pictured him at the store: *She wants glue, but I don't know which kind. To be on the safe side I will get her one of each.* Imagining him standing there in the aisle, thinking that, I felt sentimental, very much in love.

Go

I get this weird sort of rush when an ambulance comes racing down the street, and I, along with all the other drivers, quickly pull over to let the more important vehicle pass. It's as if us little cars on the side of the road are cheering, *Go! Go! You can do it! Go, important ambulance, go!* The experience invariably leaves me feeling proud and giddy.

Good to Bad Mood

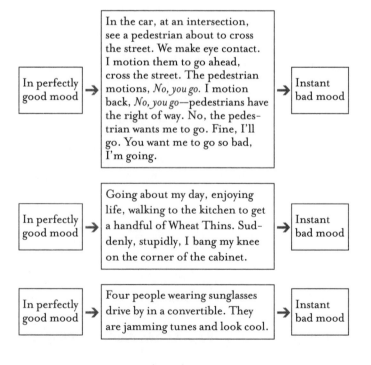

In perfectly good mood → In the car, at an intersection, see a pedestrian about to cross the street. We make eye contact. I motion them to go ahead, cross the street. The pedestrian motions, *No, you go.* I motion back, *No, you go*—pedestrians have the right of way. No, the pedestrian wants me to go. Fine, I'll go. You want me to go so bad, I'm going. → Instant bad mood

In perfectly good mood → Going about my day, enjoying life, walking to the kitchen to get a handful of Wheat Thins. Suddenly, stupidly, I bang my knee on the corner of the cabinet. → Instant bad mood

In perfectly good mood → Four people wearing sunglasses drive by in a convertible. They are jamming tunes and look cool. → Instant bad mood

GROCERIES

I do not like when our house is jam-packed full of new groceries. There is simply too much good food on hand, too many options. When we consume some of it, I feel better, as if we've done a worthwhile, necessary thing. The elimination feels satisfying, not so much in the pleasure of the eating, but in the minimization of what's available.

See also: Completion

GROCERY CART

As I was paying at the grocery store, I noticed I forgot to put what was on the bottom of my cart on the conveyor belt. It was just a single rose, wrapped in brown paper. In a split second, I had to decide:

BAD GIRL . . . . OR . . . . GOOD GIRL
Say nothing   Point to the rose
save a couple bucks   tell her I forgot
be on my way   add it to the bill

I was in a hurry and didn't really want to take the time to be good (remind me to tell you about a psychology experiment I read about where seminary students did a good deed only if they weren't in a hurry), but somehow the combination of the solitary orangey-pink rose and the doelike faces of my kids standing there pushed me into the honorable camp. Fine. I forked over the extra $2.11 and off we went. Epilogue: While unpacking the groceries at home, I realized the rose was still sitting there at the store, paid for, on the bottom of the cart.

GROUP PERSON

Taking a step class on vacation reminded me of just how much I detest group aerobic activity. *Four to the left. Four to the right. Up, down, clap, kick. Come on, everybody. Louder, I can't hear you. That's it. Again!* In general, I am not a group person. I don't go out with the girls, which I used to feel bad about, and which I know many of my friends enjoy. I prefer hanging out with one or two friends at a time. I love reading books and seeing movies,

but not within the structure of a club that meets monthly in the living room. Charise and I have formed a couple clubs over the years—we even made laminated membership cards—but we've kept the group small: her and me.

In Brownie uniform, 1973.
Last major group activity.
I lasted one session.

H

HANDWRITING

Every now and then I will try on a new handwriting style. It is like adopting a new persona. *Cool,* I'll think. But then if I am not paying close enough attention, I will forget and slip back into my natural handwriting.

HAPPINESS

I'm turning left. *Look, everyone, my blinker is on, and I'm turning left.* I am so happy to be alive, driving along, making a left turn. I'm serious. I am doing exactly what I want to be doing at this moment: existing on a Tuesday, going about my business, on my way somewhere, turning left. There is nothing disconcerting or unpleasant or unfortunate about this moment. It is exceptionally nice, plain, and perfect.

See also: Tuesday Night

HIGH SCHOOL, YEARBOOK SIGNATURES THAT SUMMARIZE

Dear Amy—
Out of all the girls I've ever met I'd have to say that you are the "Bugsiest" one I know! You've been such a good friend—always a riot to be with! We made it through two talent shows together—JJJ's and Blues Bros. were fantastik! One of the highlights of this year was prom—I had the best time at your house watching the sun rise. You were a terrific cheerleader this fall—too bad we couldn't have cheered together though!

These four years have been special and you've been a big part of it! Good luck at Tufts next year—I'll miss ya tons—but I know that I won't forget your cute smiling face!

—Love ya, C. (Bugsy!)

My dearest lover darling,
We are destined to have a hot, steamy love affair; you know it, and I know it. Frankly, though, I'm getting worried. Here it is, the end of school and we haven't yet had wild, kinky sex. There's still the summer though, so expect to be serenaded.

—Love, G.

Amy—
You are a great friend and a fun person to be around! Remember Ray? Yeah for your party. I'm psyched! Call me this summer and we'll party. I'm sure I'll call you whenever I hear of a party "southbound." Monday should be fun. Thanx again for PROM! It was great! (so was last year— under the pool table) Have fun at Tufts—Keep in touch always! Let's have a super time this summer! SCORE!

—Love always, A.

Dear Amy—
My love for you is unbounding. I pray that your summer is great and I see you at 100,000 parties. Be cool at college.

—G.

Amy—
Wow, we're about to graduate!! I've really had a good time this year LOYOLA BOUND! Talent show, prom, (memories). We definitely have many more times to party coming up this summer (I'm psyched). It sounds almost trite to say but I'm really glad we have become better friends. ALVA forever!

—Love always, L.
PS How was the econ test?

Amy,

You have to excuse the messy writing—my hand is shaking so bad due to the after effects of last night. Thanks for the invitation to the party we're going to have a great time, you've been a big part of my high school years, don't change next year, you're so sweet and cute, stay that way!!

—Love always, (ILLEGIBLE)

Dear Amy,

Carol and Billy are being shits—why don't they come up. I'm telling you those two are in love. I think she really found her man. Oh well I'm happy for her & a little jealous but I still love her. This year was excellent and I don't know how I kept my hands off you because you have the most huggable Ziggy body I've ever seen.

—Love always, T.

Ziggy,

It's all coming to an end. (JK) I'm glad we've gotten to be such good friends. We're going to have the best summer yet!!! Senior Blues forever! I can't wait till your party!!! Don't forget me next year. Keep in touch at Tufts with Tony (JK). I'm going to miss you a lot next year enough. (Sorry I'm writing in fragments) You can't forget to invite me to the wedding (even though you're not going anymore). Uh Huh! Have a great year. I'll miss you

—Love ya, N.

HOMER, ROD

I had been thinking about a couple people I went to high school with who, at the relatively young age of fourteen, fifteen, sixteen, had already discovered and made peace with their distinct, true, and unconventional selves. I had not been like this myself, and suddenly, almost out of nowhere, I regretted that I didn't *get* those people back then; that I didn't appreciate their creative offerings; that I didn't realize what tremendous inner strength and poise it must have taken to waltz around the halls with all these blobs of conforming, frightened youths huddling together. One guy in particular resurfaced in my mind. I couldn't for the life of me recall his name, but I kept thinking about him. He was tall, and he seemed to walk like a wave, up and down, up and down, with his crazy curly hair flopping with each rise and fall. He was in a band, and he was a ferocious doodler. He had a kind way about him, a winning combination of goofiness and earnestness.

Exactly two days later, it's Saturday night, and Jason and I are at a charity event. As we go into the main room to find our seating card (*Amy and Jason Rosenthal, Table 15*), I run into a friend from college who I haven't seen in years. We had recently reconnected via e-mail in a serendipitous way, but we still hadn't gotten together. The friend, Adam, introduced me to his wife, Charmane. They're at table 15, too. We catch up. Turns out Charmane and I are from the same hometown, went to the same high school a few years apart, perhaps I know her brother? Rod Homer?

Yes, Rod Homer, that's his name. Rod Homer. Tall, bouncy, confident Rod Homer.

See also: Marshmallows; Meaning; Mind, Random Things That for Some Reason Often Come Back into My; More Miles; Mr. Koch; Sensitive; Wallet, Forgotten

HOT

If something is supposed to be hot, I want it to be hot. If it is not hot, I have no interest in it. A cup of coffee, for example, should be very hot. So should those little washcloths they give you at Japanese restaurants. A lukewarm washcloth is just so depressing and wishy-washy, like a flimsy handshake. McDonald's fries are meant to be consumed right out of the deep fryer, so hot that they almost burn your mouth while you eat them and you have to do that thing where you sort of chew with your back teeth only, and with your mouth half open, while blowing on them at the same time. *Hhuh hhuh* bite, *hhuh hhuh* bite, bite. And baths, baths should be very, very hot. Because of this love of hot, I find myself constantly reheating the same cup of coffee in the microwave. Or sending my fish back with the waiter. Or getting up in the middle of dinner at home to nuke my linguine. Or coaching my kids while they cling to the edge of the tub, *oh, come on—it's not that hot, you'll get used to it.*

HUMBLING

I was out of town with the kids, talking to Jason on the phone. I was thinking, *He's really missing me.* I imagined that talking to me on the phone was a high point of his day, and how happy he must be to be having this conversation. But then wait, what's that I'm hearing in the background, that gentle *click click click?* Sure sounds like keyboard pitter-patter to me. Is he actually typing on his computer?

J, are you typing right now?
Uh, yeah.

Table	
TRAVELING	
You Say	**How It Sounds**
I'm going overseas.	Sounds like you're going to the Orient, or somewhere really far away.
I'm going abroad.	Has junior-year-in-college undertones.

(continued)

TRAVELING	
You Say	**How It Sounds**
I'll be out of the country.	Sounds like you're a spy. Mysterious. Ambiguous. A nameless place, somewhere people go to engage in covert operations.
I'm going to Europe.	Well, la-di-da, good for you. Pretentious.
I'm going to France.	Fine, but compels people to say, "I see London, I see France, I see _____'s underpants."

HUNGER PREVENTION

It's not just that we eat if we're hungry, but we eat if we're worried that we will be hungry. For example, let's say I'm going to a seven o'clock movie—that's right smack in the middle of dinnertime. I won't be hungry at five-thirty or six, but I must prevent the hunger that will inevitably occur halfway through the movie and take care of it now. I MUST EAT IN ADVANCE OF MY HUNGER. Thus, I grab a sandwich or bowl of pasta, eat it with minimal pleasure, but acknowledge that I have done something necessary. I have come at my hunger from the back door and eliminated any possible future hunger discomfort.

HUSBAND

Jason and I were fixed up on a blind date, by my dad's best friend, John. When I opened my front door and saw him, I knew there was something between us. By the end of our merlot and rigatoni, I knew he was the one. Fifty-two weeks later, he knew. I like how when his sister Michel phones him he just answers *yep* or *uh-huh* and then she either talks and he occasionally goes *alrighty then* or, more characteristically, says nothing at all. I like how they always call each other during exciting TV events like the Grammys or *The Sopranos'* season finale or some Freeview Prince concert on satellite and just sit on the phone together in total silence, sharing the show from their respective city posts. I like that he's had the same best friend since he was three. (Hey, Dave.) I like that he's a good dancer and a surprisingly good jacks player. I like how he barely ever annoys me. I like how we dine at restaurants—either on stools at the bar instead of waiting an hour and a half for a table, or if we do sit at a table, we'll sit next to each other instead of across. I like how he looks when he's making a toast—thoughtful, composed, handsome, you know, like a real gentleman. I like how he laughs when he really laughs hard, like during the Will Ferrell streaking scene in *Old School.* I like how he's forgiving when I shut down and retreat inward. I like how he doesn't give me a hard time about my heap of clothes in the closet, though we both know I have less tolerance for his harmless, scattered piles. I like how he doesn't make me feel bad about my lack of enthusiasm for important adult things like politics and Quicken. I like that I don't mind how he smells when he sweats. I like that when we Wght, he tends to have a point, and he makes it skillfully and convincingly. I like how he holds a skillet. I like his hands, they Wt good with mine.

I

IDENTITY

Experiment: How might I look as a *Wanted* poster?

Drawing based on father's description to police sketch artist.

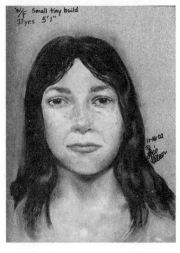

Drawing based on husband's description to police sketch artist.

IMPROVISATION AT CONCERTS

I go to a concert, a band I really love. The band plays the first few bars of my absolutely favorite song, but then . . . what's that? They're altering it, improvising. The band thinks this is refreshing and artful, a welcome deviation, a prize for attending. But I am irked and disappointed they didn't play it just as I've enjoyed it on the CD all these years.

See also: Comfort in the Expected

INFINITY

Justin came home from school with the announcement that he had just learned what even and odd numbers were. *Okay,* I said. *So tell me: What's infinity, even or odd?* I certainly didn't have an answer in mind; I posed it only as a fun, unanswerable kind of question. He thought about it for a moment, then concluded: *Mom, infinity is an 8 on its side, so it is an even number.*

[intermission]

Introducing a Friend to a Friend

Sometimes you have a friend and think, *She would really like my other friend so-and-so,* and you introduce them, and sure enough, they become friends, they totally hit it off, and there you are, demoted to background buddy.

[1]

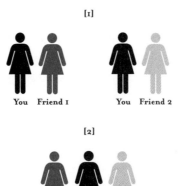

You   Friend 1   You   Friend 2

[2]

Friend 1   You   Friend 2

[3]

Friend 1   Friend 2

[4]

You

J

Jacket Bio

There is a direct correlation between how much a book moves me and how often I flip to the author's photo. Midsentence I will feel a pull to return to that photo/bio on the back flap. *Take me at once to the man who wrote such a splendid thought!* The photo serves as a sort of home base. And at progressive intervals, the photo will seem more and more revealing, more and more interesting. Invariably, I will find myself idealizing and envying this person and his three-sentence life as captured in the bio. He is the author of several novels, a memoir, and, most recently, a collection of short stories. *He is professor of English at Berkeley. He lives on the beach with his wife and dog Hemingway.* Oh, how complete. Impressive. Idyllic. And complication-free. Only his close friends know that his recent novel ended up in the five-bucks-and-under bin; that he is in the midst of a major lawsuit with the beach house contractor; that his wife, two years before, was his kid's nanny. But for the rest of us, the casual admirers, the main thing, the important thing, is that the author's jacket photo credits Nick Hornby as the photographer, and one can only imagine the exclusive literary soiree that produced this sweet little digital memento.

Jason

J-A-S-O-N. J—July. A—August. S—September. O—October. N—November. We met in July. We got engaged in November.

See also: Dreams; Husband

Jobs I Could Never Do

I would abhor being a professional mover; I would just whine and complain the whole time. Nor would I make a very good Buckingham  Palace guard; I get the giggles way too easily and/or smirk at inappropriate times (while reprimanding my kids; upon hearing tragic news).

K

KIDS' MEALS ON FLIGHTS

I never remember to pre-order the kids' meals, it never even occurs to me, until I see the flight attendant prancing down the aisle with fun, colorful trays for children who are not mine.

KLASSY

I saw a car whose license plate read: KLASSY. It was a Cadillac. I think it's easy to put the guy down—and you can just picture what he looks like, can't you? So easy to say, *man, what a loser, how tacky.* But it's all about context. If an old, pudgy, gold necklace—wearing fellow gets behind the wheel of his Klassy Cadillac, it seems cheesy. But if it was, say, Beck driving that very same Klassy Cadillac, it would suddenly be cool in a kitschy, in-on-the-joke way. This isn't exactly fair. But is there any way to get around it? Perhaps a more enlightened person would have glanced over at the Klassy geezer and thought, *Cool, good for him.* Or better yet, had no judgments at all.

L

LACY UNDERSHIRTS

When I got engaged, my mother took me shopping for what was once upon a time called a trousseau, a gift of garments mothers traditionally sent their virgin daughters off with as they began their new lives as wives. It was sweet and old-fashioned and unnecessary and so my mom. It was there in the lingerie department that she held up these lacy, shoulder-padded undershirt things and said, *You will definitely need a couple of these.* I had never worn—let alone seen—a lacy, shoulder-padded undershirt thing before. But I figured my mom knew what she was doing, and that when I got married, perhaps mere minutes after exchanging vows, I would be a different person. I couldn't quite picture who that person was, but I imagined that the married Amy would be more grown-up, more put together, more better—basically, that I would suddenly have a pressing need for lacy, shoulder-padded undershirt things. After seven years of marriage and seven years of still looking at those undershirts with the tags still on, I finally put them in a bag to be donated to charity. It was bittersweet, but also there was a sense of relief: I no longer had to sit around wondering what I was doing wrong, why my married-glamorous self refused to present itself, why I wasn't getting into bed every night with freshly shaven legs and glistening, sweet-smelling skin from jasmine bath oils. Being yourself seems like the most effortless thing in the world—duh, who else are you going to be? But it's deceiving, tricky, a summons laden with meandering and failed attempts—and then at last, so wondrously simple. Like the riddle, *floccinaucinihilipilification is the longest word in the English language—can you spell it?* I may have thought I wanted to be a red-silk-nightie kind of wife. But it turns out that the right answer for me is I feel sexier in boy-short undies and a Mr. Bubble T-shirt. I-T.

LAUNDRY BASKET

I'm getting undressed. I don't feel like folding my pants or hanging them up. I'd rather they be dirty so I can put them in the laundry basket. I check out the legs closely, the seat—bummer, they look pretty clean. But then, wait, the bottom of the legs are dirty—very dirty in fact. Excellent, I can legitimately toss them in the basket, I'm not just being lazy.

LEAVES

My friend Scott's son looked at the leaves twirling around outside and said, *Look, Dad—the leaves are playing with each other.*

LEAVING A TIP

When leaving a tip at the counter, I often do so with exaggerated gestures, or take a bit longer than necessary to place the dollar in the dish, just to make sure they know what a nice and generous customer I am.

LETTERS

The letters *a, e, g,* and *s* seem nice; *k, v,* and *x* seem meaner.

See also: Ayn Rand

LIFE

The same two words, albeit in reverse order, sum it all up:

Home nursing
Nursing home

LIFE AS CAPSULIZED ON PUBLIC RADIO MORNING NEWS

Alex Dryer died today. He was an NBC anchor for forty years. It's forty-nine degrees today and sunny skies. This is WBEZ Chicago.

LIFE AS PRESET MENU

Menu A

Charming
Good at Ping-Pong
Bad speller
A lot of moles
Content with career
Optimistic
Car breaks down a lot

Menu B

Fabulous piano player
Quite unattractive
Rich
Well-behaved children
Allergic to chocolate
Grating laugh
Nice garden

Menu C

Friends who adore you
Chronic insomnia
Look great in skimpy underwear
Color-blind
Bilingual
Motivated
Bad kisser
Will live a long life

Choose one. No substitutions please.

Limousine

Very few individuals are able to walk by a parked limousine without comment.

Lollipop Tree

Our friends woke up early one morning and tied hundreds of lollipops to their tree in the backyard. They invited our kids, and a few lucky others, to join their family in a celebration in honor of their lollipop tree, which, as anyone could see, had just come into full bloom. We watched for a few, sacred minutes those eight or so children shrieking in delight and wonder, picking lollipops off the tree.

Lost Item

When I can't find something in my house—a pair of jeans, let's say, or even something small and stupid like a Sharpie marker—the first thought that runs through my head is, *I can't believe the cleaning woman took that!* For years, she has been nothing but loyal and trustworthy, handing me nickels and pennies retrieved from the washing machine, for God's sake, but still, for that split second, I think this has all been some kind of convoluted scheme so one day she could abscond with my pants. Of course, I always find the misplaced item a moment later, and then shake my head at myself while releasing a disgusted, guttural *hm*, ashamed that I could have even thought to internally accuse her.

LOVE

If you really love someone, you want to know what they ate for lunch or dinner without you. *Hi, sweetie, how was your day, what did you have for lunch?* Or if your mate was out of town on business: *How was your trip, did the meeting go well, what did you do for dinner?* Jason will stumble home in the wee hours from a bachelor party, and as he crawls into bed I'll pry myself from sleep long enough to mumble, *how was the party, how was the restaurant beforehand?* The meal that has no bearing on the relationship appears to be breakfast. I can love you and not know that when you were in Cincinnati last Wednesday you had yogurt and a bagel.

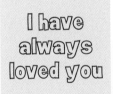

Which typeface gives you the impression I really mean it?

LOWS

Age 3: Friends Christie and Tommy move away.

Age 5: Get sick night before I'm supposed to go on airplane and visit grandmother.

Age 14: Family moves second semester freshman year.

Age 14: At bull session at overnight camp, A. says she hates my brown bathing suit, it's ugly.

Age 16: Car accident.

Age 16: Speeding ticket.

Age 16: Speeding ticket.

Age 18: Have a party when parents go out of town. Get caught. Grounded for entire summer.

Age 18: T. has big graduation party and doesn't invite me.

Age 21: Grandmother dies.

Age 22: D. and I break up.

Age 24: Ellen killed.

Age 25: E. says nasty things to me on the phone and makes me cry.

Age 26: Offered dream job; husband doesn't want to move to Portland; no choice but to turn it down.

Age 27: Complications with first pregnancy.

Age 27: Fired by M. Seven months pregnant with first child at the time.

Age 32: Sister-in-law dies during childbirth.

Age 34: Lump in neck. Biopsy.

Age 35: Computer crashes.

Age 35: Father has open-heart surgery.

Age 36: September 11.

Age 37: Boat accident. Miles injured.

Age 37: Leave CD case containing favorite CDs on the security belt at airport.

LUCKY

In an online column I was writing, I devised a sort of cyber scavenger hunt. One of the instructions was for readers to go to google.com, plug in *Lucky Charms*, and tell me the first listing that pops up. When I created this game, I had no idea what the Google search would reveal—I had come up with this scavenger hunt idea away from my computer—but I just thought, *Okay, I'll do a Google thing, have them plug in something fun, pop culturey, something smiley and smirky. Let's see . . . Lucky Charms cereal. Perfect.* I figured this would surely lead to some magically delicious Web page featuring the little leprechaun character.

It was only when I started hearing back from readers who had proudly found all the scavenger hunt items that I learned what the search coughed up. The first listing was a link to CNN.com, reporting on the gentleman who invented Lucky Charms. He had recently been killed in a car accident, along with his wife, on their way to visit their daughter, who, horrifically enough, was in a coma and dying in the hospital.

At this point, I could have altered the Google question for the game, but I felt that this devastating, absurd, unfathomable, true story was meant to be read. That such an ending would come to the creator of a cereal named Lucky Charms seemed to be yet another glaring example of how curiously beautiful-tragic-ridiculous-poignant-dreadful-happy-sad it all is.

See also: Wabi-Sabi

Table

CEREAL SLOGANS	
Lucky Charms	*They're magically delicious.*
Frosted Flakes	*They're grrrrrrreat.*
Rice Krispies	*Snap. Crackle. Pop.*
Trix	*Silly rabbit, Trix are for kids.*
Kix	*Mother-tested. Kid-approved.*
Cocoa Puffs	*I'm coo-coo for Cocoa Puffs.*

Lucky (Versus Smart)

A gentleman at dinner the other night said, in response to a comment about his success and abundant wealth, *you know, I'd rather be lucky than smart.* I used to like that expression till I heard him say it, at which point it became clear to me how smug and full-of-it that line is. He really meant the exact opposite when he said it. It's an attempt to be modest, but really, what's being conveyed is: *I am smart enough to know this expression, smart enough to use it in this conversation so you think I'm being humble, but deep down you and I both know that my astounding success can be traced and attributed to my brilliant mind. This success is my destiny, luck or no luck.*

M

Magazines

I cannot keep up with all the magazines. I want to. I want to read them all. I want to ingest them, preferably in one gulp, so then I can move on to my wobbly tower of nightstand books, my real reading. But they just keep coming at you, the magazines do, every damn month, or worse, every week. They refuse to let us catch up, catch our breath, be done, have closure. You've got *People* with its irresistible celebrity gossip (Uma snagged a hot new beau! Sandra Bullock and Matthew McConaughey spottings!), and *Newsweek* with its *Perspective* quote page up front and book and movie reviews in back, and all those brilliant *New Yorker* cartoons, and *Reader's Digest*'s latest survival tale (an avalanche! a shark attack! trapped under a fallen tree, in a cave, on a mountain, for eight, sixteen, eleven days), and my husband's subscriptions to *Rolling Stone* and *Esquire* don't help things any (both of which keep lobbing these great multi-page profile pieces at me: Liz Phair, Bill Murray, that superstar chef outside of Barcelona), and who can resist the "Readings" section of *Harper's* or the consistent right-on-ness of *The Onion* and the zeitgeist pearl I always extract from the bundle: The Sunday *Magazine* (Google these big stories: meta, Sofia Coppola, anything by Lisa Belkin, for an accurate distillation of the current sociocultural vibe), and I can always be seduced by a good *Utne Reader, Bon Appétit,* or *Entertainment Weekly.*

The only magazines that never tempt me are the time line-y, rehashing, year-in-review issues.

The only magazines I can read without a shade of guilt are those I find at the dentist's office or hair salon, because I never have—and would never think to bring—a book with me. It was at the latter locale that I happened upon A. A. Gill's restaurant review (rant) in *Vanity Fair* (August 2003), which in my book ties with Brian Frazier's back-page pieces in *Esquire* for freshest—in both senses—magazine voice.

The only magazines I don't chuck are the ones I am in.

See also: Completion

Magic Wand

When they were little, Justin and Miles would frequently ask me—and they were completely sincere—*Mom, when you get your magic wand, will you change us into tigers?* And I would say, *Yes, when I get a real magic wand, I will be happy to change you into tigers.* This thrilled them to no end. They would talk about what life would be like when they were tigers. They would be able to jump higher. They would be able to run faster. They wouldn't have to nap. I played along in a very serious way, because I so badly wanted to be able to make this happen for them, if only for a minute. How they wished and marveled and believed. One day we went to a costume store on a quest to find not a pretend magic wand but *a real magic wand*. We found one that looked pretty authentic. The boys could hardly contain themselves in the car ride home. I remember standing in their room, holding the wand out, saying that if it worked, I would want them to come back home for dinner, that I would feed their tiger selves but then I'd change them back into little boys for bedtime. When my "One, two, three" failed to produce sparks, and they saw that they were still standing there the same as ever, I felt that I had let them down in the hugest, most irreparable way.

Man from Egypt

From journal, August 17, 1987:

Cab home. Nice older man from Egypt. He said I was the first one to guess his native country ("Italy? Greece? Israel? Egypt?" "Yes!"). "Twenty-two is the best age—you remember that. You remember that in years to come that your cabdriver said this." I felt bittersweet by his kindness. "Good night, Amy. Good luck with everything. Have a good life," he said.

Marshmallows

Charise and I declared a particular week the Week of the Marshmallow. There was no logic to this; it simply emerged. As the week unfolded, these things happened:

1. At the grocery store I told Justin he could pick out one dessert for dinner that night. He really agonized over his decision, walking up and down the cookie aisle, the candy aisle, looking at pastries. And then, totally out of the blue, he presented me with a bag of marshmallows.

2. While on vacation my three-year-old niece was yearning for home. She told her mom, *I just want to go to our house and eat marshmallows.*

3. For the first time ever in our eleven years of marriage, and with absolutely no knowledge of my word of the week, Jason came home from the store with a jar of Marshmallow Fluff.

Did I somehow will these marshmallow events to occur? Or did I just notice (and otherwise would not have) what would have occurred regardless? Like that game you can play at a stadium—call *red* and all the red shirts pop out; call *yellow* and . . . —my vision was skewed. Back when Jason and I were crafting bracelets out of antique buttons, I was always finding cool buttons on the sidewalk. *Such a beautiful button, just lying there, I can't wait to show J. . .* But aha, once we stopped making the bracelets, the sidewalk in turn stopped presenting me with these stray gems; I don't think I've found a roadside button since. Evidently, if you put yourself on high marshmallow alert, high button alert, high injustice alert, high whatever alert, the world will gladly accommodate you.

MEANING

I am working on letting go of trying to find meaning where there probably is none. For example, I stepped outside and at once saw a license plate that read AMY1429; my birthday is April 29—4/29—so except for the 1, the license plate was perfect, and surely a sign of something, I thought. And this: I was at the video store picking out a movie for the kids, and as I walked down the aisle, my backpack accidentally knocked a video off the rack. I picked it up. *Adventures in Babysitting. Hmmm. Interesting. The children are meant to watch this tonight,* I thought—as if this movie had some important message to impart, one that would alter the course of my children's lives and make them better people. That same week, at the drugstore, I was trying to choose a hair color from the rows and rows of nearly identical shades. The boxes were uniformly stacked, except for one sole box that happened to be jetting out a tad. *This is the one,* I thought, eyeing the model's hair more closely. *A bit blonder than I would have chosen, but I trust the gesture just the same.* And I immediately took #211 Ginger Zing to the counter.

FINDING MEANING IN LICENSE PLATES

Jason took an unusual, alternate route. "Where are you going?" I asked. "Don't worry," he said. "I used to do this shortcut all the time with my dad when I was a kid. I remember the way perfectly." At that moment a car pulled in front of us . . .

Jace was his nickname growing up.

I was thinking about staying true to my own thing, just doing what I do, what I like to do, what I do best, not worrying about what others are doing. Making comparisons is useless. They are them. I am me. Then I saw . . .

Yes, exactly. Be Amy. Who else?

Jason and I went to a sushi restaurant on the night they happened to be serving a delicacy—shots of electric baby eel. Feeling brave, Jason ordered one. They looked like shiny, green, thrashing angel-hair noodles. There were about twenty of them. Occasionally one would jump to the top of the shot glass. I watched him down it. Jason said he could feel a couple of the eels trying to shimmy back up his throat. Our mutual and immediate reaction to all this was: The kids would have loved to see this, particularly the boys, who were still talking about the chocolate-covered grasshoppers we brought home (and which they ate) from a Mexican restaurant two years before. So Sunday morning we shared the eel news with them. This was just about the coolest thing ever to them. Justin was particularly captivated and proceeded to tell anyone who would listen to the story of Daddy and the electric green eel. He would tell it with such detail and drama: "Okay, so there was a little glass, about this big . . ." A couple days later, while I was driving home, I was thinking about it again, about how exciting this story was to the boys, how in awe they were, how impressed and proud of their dad they were, and how fun it was for me to watch Justin retell the story. I looked up . . .

EEL48

On the way to Charise's, I was thinking about a private-eye experiment I wanted to conduct for this book. The gist was to have a detective get photographs of Jason and me from a distance, walking out of a restaurant—documenting our *monogamy*. I was debating whether to stage the whole thing—tell the detective over the phone that I suspected my husband was having an affair, send photos of him and his supposed mistress (me)—or just go speak with the guy in person, tell him the truth, that it was more the standard procedure and black-and-white catch-them-from-a-distance snapshot-photo style I was after. I kept going back and forth. *Stage it. Be up front. Stage it. Be up front.* At the stoplight right before turning to her house, I looked up . . .

I C THRU U

I e-mailed my old high-school boyfriend to ask him if I might interview him for this book. Our anniversary way back when was March 16, or 316 as we referred to it; it became a number that we saw everywhere for years—even friends and family members would comment on it. While we had kept in touch sporadically over the years, there had never been a reason to communicate for work-related reasons, that is, until this day when I e-mailed him. Later that afternoon I was driving the kids somewhere and looked over to see the license plate . . .

WERK 316

MESSAGES

Each time I go to play my messages, I think, *I need to put a little pad of paper right here by the answering machine.* I never do it. Instead, I keep cramming phone numbers and notes into the tiny, insufficient margins of the operating manual that we keep on the shelf by the phone.

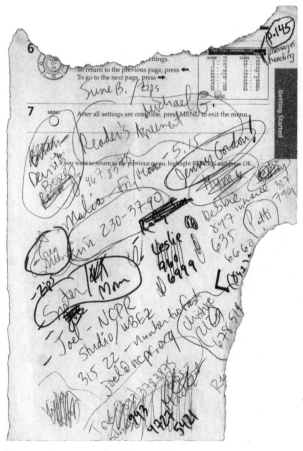

Messages written on page of operating manual.

Mind, Random Things That for Some Reason Often Come Back into My

AGE 16
During my last year of overnight camp, our cabin picking out matching T-shirts with cabin mates (a tradition after our weeklong canoe trip). I had it in my head that gray shirts with red iron-on letters would look great. Standing there in the store, I said very calmly that I was going to get that color combo, but it didn't necessarily mean everyone else had to. I felt like I wasn't being bossy about it, just certain about that choice for me. The whole group did end up getting gray/red shirts. Was I being bossy? Or was I just being confidently assertive?

AGE 20
David telling me to put people in all the photos that I took while I was abroad junior year, that I might not think so at the time, but when I got home, all the tourist stuff would be dull without any humans in it.

AGE 27
L. telling me that you can't use big words with your children, and despite the fact that I was a brand-new mom, instinctively I knew that I didn't agree, that I wouldn't use lowest-common-denominator speak, that their little minds could gradually absorb the gist of big words.

AGE 25
M. telling me that in general I talk pretty loudly. We were in some kind of store at the time, maybe a video store. I never knew I spoke loudly, but from that point on, whenever I've heard someone speaking loudly, I've wondered if that's how I sound.

AGE 15
My driver's ed teacher asking which is safer: driving close to the other cars on the highway or keeping your distance. I guessed the former, thinking there was safety in numbers—my teen world enforced the group/clique theory, and I figured it was the same with cars. Only later, in college, did I discover the fascinating concept of individuality, of driving solo.

More Miles

I saw this sign on the back of a truck:

> **MORE MILES**
> **BETTER PAY**

I read it with an implicit *or* between the two lines. The sign was saying to me, Here are the two, diametrically opposed spectrums of your life: more time with Miles (and Justin and Paris) or more time to write.

Movies

I always want to see what happens after the movie is technically over. I want an update on the couple that fell in love in Dolby Surround Sound, to see how they're doing post-euphoria. Have they begun fighting over small increments of time? (*You said you'd be home at seven-fifteen. It's seven-twenty.*) Or in *Ransom*, for example, after they get their son back in the end, I want to see what their family life is like. When they're sitting around the breakfast table, do they reminisce, *can you believe you were chained up to a bed for a week?*

Mr. Koch

Not too long ago, I sent some material off to an editor in Ohio. In the package, I included a copy of a poem that I love, one I had first read in *The New Yorker* a couple of years prior. I am not a poetry aficionado; I don't even understand that many poems. But Mr. Koch's poem I love, and I refer to it often. I wanted to share it with my Ohio colleague because I thought he, too, might love it, and in turn like me a bit more for introducing it to him, in the same way one feels fondly toward the friend who clued him in on, say, Elliott Smith, or the movie *Strangers in Good Company*.

A few days later the Ohio gentleman told me that when my package arrived, he promptly leafed through it, read the poem, and then dashed out to meet a friend for lunch. When he arrived at the restaurant, he saw that his friend had brought along an out-of-town guest to join them. Now, of course I am going to tell you that the guest turned out to be the poet, Mr. Koch.

YOU WANT A SOCIAL LIFE, WITH FRIENDS

You want a social life, with friends,
A passionate love life as well
To work hard every day. What's true
Is of these three you may have two
And two can pay you dividends
But never may have three

There isn't time enough, my friends—
Though dawn begins, yet midnight ends—
To find the time to have love, work, and friends.
Michelangelo had feeling
For Vittoria and Ceiling
But did he go to parties at day's end?

Homer nightly went to banquets
Wrote all day but had no lockets
Bright with pictures of his Girl.
I know one who loves and parties
And has done so since his thirties
But writes hardly anything at all.

Poem by Kenneth Koch

N

NAILS

Having a glass of wine inevitably results in me biting and picking at my nails.

NAMES AS THEY SEEMINGLY INFLUENCE ONE'S CHOSEN PROFESSION

Art Spiegelman	Artist/cartoonist
Amby Burfoot	Runner/writer who wrote book about running
Sarah Vowell	Writer
DD Smalley	Creator of the Hyde Park Miniature Museum
Francine Prose	Writer
Meg Musick	Artist who makes bags/purses out of album covers
Michael Green	Environmental activist
Henry Calvin Goodrich	Wealthy entrepreneur who ended up donating his fortune to charity
Dr. Cherry	Gynecologist
Mrs. Gotchalk	Teacher

Napkins

I found a 1950s handbook titled *Folding Table Napkins* in the car. I could not for the life of me figure out where this had come from. In a matter of seconds, I ran through all conceivable options: Was it mine and I'd just forgotten I had it? Had it been in the crevice between the seats for years, left by a friend or a valet driver? Was my husband having an affair with a party planner? Turned out that Jason had picked it up for me as a gift at a thrift shop.

Needlepoint

I had stated the following in a column I wrote:

> *The greatest piece of needlepoint art ever would be one that admitted in meticulously stitched lettering* ——————

I TRULY HATED EVERY MINUTE OF THIS!

> *If I ever saw that at a craft fair, or featured in a mail-order catalog as a cute little throw pillow, I would buy it in a second, and pay good money for it.*

A reader promptly offered to needlepoint one for me.

Actual needlepoint.

Nice Words

Soup and *pond* are both such nice words, *pond* especially. You think: small, quiet, calm, clear. And the ducks.

Nimiety

I can think of nothing less necessary than the cereal Froot Loops with marshmallows.

Nipple

Nipple is a funny word. Maybe it's because you can't help but picture one, and because it's at once erotic and clinical sounding and so anatomically dot dot specific. Even saying the word—your lips push out a *puh* and then your tongue goes *lllll*—is funny. *Nipple.* The idea of nipples on boys always seemed goofy—those flat things aren't *nipple* nipples. And now I'm remembering, as kids we used to giggle in the presence of a box of Cheese Nips crackers. *Hee, hee, snicker, snicker. It's sexual but we don't know why!* Once you introduce breast-feeding into the repertoire, nipples take on a double persona: sometimes provocative headlights, other times just handy, elastic, marvelously functional gadgets.

Nose Job

I can never tell if a woman has had a nose job. Jason always says, *you're telling me you couldn't tell? It was so obvious.* I just assume that was her nose.

Note

When someone mails something to me—like a copy of an article, for example—it's so much better when they include a quick note, or even just a Post-it. *Here's the article I was talking about at dinner the other night. Talk to you soon.* Otherwise I'm left searching the envelope going, *that's kinda lame, no note, how impersonal.* Even just a quick *hope you like it! Love, me* does the trick and confirms our friendly connection.

NOTE ON AIR CONDITIONER

The hotel housekeeping keeps putting our air conditioner on, and Jason and I keep turning it off. We prefer the breeze and fresh air from the windows. By the second or third time they turn the air on, we decide to leave a note on the air-conditioning unit itself so they can't miss it. The unit is affixed high on the wall, so I have to stand on a chair to leave the note: *Please leave off. Do not turn on.* I draw the circle/slash symbol in case they don't exactly understand. We return later to find the note has been moved slightly to the side, and the air is, yet again, on. This seems incredibly funny to us, imagining them seeing the note and deciding that we were just leaving them a note to say, you know, hi, all the way up there on top of the air-conditioning unit.

NOTHING

Death is the ultimate nothing. We are petrified of this nothing, yet we spend a great portion of our lives trying to create a state of near-nothingness. We spend the day hacking away at our to-do lists so finally, when the dishes are done and the kids are in bed, we can sit on the couch and do nothing.

Doing nothing feels natural, and we easily slip into it. Doing nothing often involves some kind of watching: Sitting at a café or in a park people watching. Being the passenger in a car, watching the trees or lines on the highway go by. Watching nothing on TV.

Movies are ideal because they combine doing something

with doing nothing. You have gone out, but you do not have to do or say anything. The people in the movies are doing everything for you, expending themselves; nothing is required of you at all. That is why—unlike going to a party or a wedding—going to the movies never feels like a social obligation. On the occasions where we do have to participate, to do more than nothing, it is desirable to have a glass of wine to soften all the everything.

Nuances of Words

There's a parking garage I often pass on Wabash that has a sign that says: NO ONE TOUCHES YOUR CAR BUT YOU. All of the other garages say SELF PARK. Of course, these are the exact same kind of parking garages, but one makes you feel privileged and empowered, and the other is sort of saying, *We're lazy*—YOU *park your damn car.*

They've recently changed the *one size fits all* tags to say *one size fits most.* I think this new version is rather awful. *One size fits all* was inclusive: *Hey, everybody, we're in this together.* It was also meaningless in a good way, innocuous, generic. But the language of this new version is halting. *Fits most.* That clearly rubs it into the excluded minority.

We called to make reservations at a hot restaurant, and instead of saying, *Sorry, we're booked,* they said, *We're completely committed tonight.* The *booked* response makes one grumpy, but this *committed* language, that's a totally new angle, never heard a restaurant say that before. I hung up going, *Yes, these are honorable restaurant people, they are committed to their patrons, they've made a pact and are standing by it. I support that.*

Nun

A friend sat next to a nun on a plane. He asked her what she missed most. "Wearing blue jeans," she replied.

O

OFFERING NAME AS A WITNESS

While driving to work, I saw this woman pull out right in front of another driver, and the two cars immediately crashed. After driving one block, I turned around to go back to the scene to offer my name as a witness. I did this partly because I felt it was my civic duty, and partly because I wanted to chat about the collision. *What was that lady thinking?! I mean, I saw the whole thing. . . .*

OFFICE DEPOT

If I step foot in Office Depot I can't not buy something. The last unnecessary purchase was a WILL RETURN sign with the clock and movable plastic hands. I thought it would be fun to hang in the house somewhere. I finally threw it out yesterday.

OLDER COUPLE

I saw this old couple—attractive, well-groomed, but old, in their eighties—sitting down at Starbucks the other afternoon. I couldn't help but stare at them; I was intrigued by their old-ness, their presence, as old people, at Starbucks. I suddenly felt like it would be okay to go up to them and converse about their oldness. I would ask them if they look at each other and say, *can you believe how old we are? we were once young, and now we are old.* I imagined them naked. I was curious if coffee tasted any different once you got old, or if it was pretty much the same pleasure it had always been. There was a muffin on their table, and he was reading the paper; he was dressed up, wearing a jacket and tie, as old(er) gentlemen often do. I imagined Jason old, and wondered if, even though he is not this way now, he would wear a jacket and tie once he got really old, and I hoped not because I don't think I would find that attractive. I hoped he would still wear his brown corduroy shirt with the button-down snaps, and his cute form-fitting sweaters, particularly the one with the stripes that I like.

See also: Photos, Old; Sexy

OPENING

I have no patience for figuring out how a package of cookies or a manila pouch in the mail or a bag of lettuce opens. It's not really even a matter of patience, though; that implies that at first I want to find the designated opening. I simply dive right in, tear into it, never occurs to me to take a moment to access the opening options but soon lose interest in it. I only realize after the fact that, yes, right here, there is a nice perforated line or convenient ziplock seal or *tear here* arrow, which would have made the opening of the package/pouch/lettuce much easier and much neater. My world is one where lettuce escapes out the side of the bag, and clumps of white fluff ooze from the padded envelope onto the counter and floor.

OPINION, FRAGILE FOUNDATION OF STRONG

The two people laughing and drinking and carrying on at the next table are annoying, stupid, childishly conspiring, and clearly beneath you, until they invite you over to join them.

OPTIMIST

My dad is such an optimist that when his watch battery ran out, his immediate reaction was, *well, FINally.*

ORDER NUMBER

I never write down the order number when ordering from a catalog even though I pretend to do so when the salesperson says, *Do you have a pen handy? I'm going to give you your order number now.*

OTHER PEOPLE

It's hard to accept that other people's lives are as full and real and *now* as yours. You look at someone and sort of think, against your intellectual knowing better, that they have a less complex life, they're able to flit about, their lives aren't clogged with the same kind of pressing deadlines, they don't really have cousins like you have cousins, they are free tonight, of course they are free, or if they have plans they can easily break them to be with you. Our lives just feel so impossibly big to us; we're breathing versions of that Saul Steinberg poster, where New York is in the foreground, prominent and massive and drawn in colored-pencil detail, and the other states and Asia and Africa are tiny lumps fading into the horizon.

This egocentric/inner bigness is precisely why we have conversations like this with our friends:

You: *I tried calling you this morning.*

Them: *Well, you know I've got that Pilates class I'm teaching on Thursday mornings, and then I had to run over to . . .*

You (thinking): *I have no idea what you're talking about. What Pilates class? I have not memorized the intricacies of your daily schedule. I do not even know if there are one or two* n*'s in your last name.*

And it is precisely why people leave their phone number so quickly on other people's answering machines; they've said the number so many times that they think everyone else in the world is as familiar with it as they are. The number has become synonymous with their identity: *Surely my phone number/me is as prominent in your brain as it/I is/am in mine.*

It is precisely why the tiresome phrase *you know me,* followed by a characteristic, habit, or preference of some kind, sounds so self-involved. *Oh, you know me, I don't care where we go to dinner.*

And it is precisely why you think everyone is looking at you and your lopsided, Novocained mouth, when in fact, not only is the droop indiscernible, but there is not even a single gaze directed your way; you're filler at best. You're one of the endless chunks of extraneous, dispensable flesh flurrying about in the wings of the next person's (equally delusional) center stage.

P

PALINDROME

I am overly enamored with the palindrome: Won Ton, Not Now.

See also: Wordplays

PARIS

I was going through a massive sack of letters I had sent my boyfriend during my junior year abroad in Paris, which was nearly twenty years ago. I was thrilled that he still had the letters, though not shocked: There were simply too many of them to just casually pitch. It was funny to receive the package, with a quickly scribbled *Here you go* note on his business letterhead, all that passion and *je t'aime*-ing traveling through time and space to arrive at my middle-aged doorstep via FedEx. I wanted to reread the letters because I knew that I had thoroughly chronicled my day-to-day thoughts and experiences, and because it was such an important time in my life—I always viewed that year as an awakening of sorts—I thought I might be able to pinpoint (to the day!) my stunning emotional and intellectual growth, to actually see it unfolding from one powderblue airmail letter to the next. But after going through a couple dozen missives, pretty much what I learned was: (1) "Thoroughly chronicling" makes for a hell of a boring read and is best kept to dispensable journal writing. (2) It is painfully embarrassing to reread what I wrote; I sounded so— what's the word?—so *up!* all the time. (3) Despite the exceedingly detailed and lengthy nature of the letters, there is no real documentation of alleged awakening. And (4) apparently that year I cooked a lot of stir-fry.

PARKING SPOT

I would rather take the extra two minutes to maneuver into a tight and awkward parking spot that is a couple feet closer to my destination than take the big, wide-open spot a few cars down.

PARKING TICKET

There is that moment when I get a parking ticket when I want to be like *Screw that, I'm not touching that stupid ticket,* and just leave it on my windshield to spite the cop. But then, next stop in my train of thought: *The cop isn't even here to see me ignore the ticket, so what's the use, and not only that, but I'll look like a total idiot driving around with it flapping against the windshield wiper.*

Experiment: Contest Parking Ticket on Grounds of Karma
(see pages 156–160)

NOTICE OF VIOLATION

City of Chicago Department of Revenue
www.cityofchicago.org
P.O. Box 88292, Chicago, Illinois 60680-1292
(312) 744-PARK (7275); TTY (312) 744-7277 (If Hearing Impaired)
1-800-336-2446 (FOR AREA CODES 217,309,618, AND 815 ONLY)

NOTICE: You must be the registered owner of the plate on this notice to request a hearing or obtain information - A photo ID is required.
To The Registered Owner or Lessee of: PAS C367841 IL

You have failed to respond to the following Violation Notice(s)
WITHIN 14 DAYS OF THIS NOTICE YOU MUST
• **EITHER PAY THE APPLICABLE FINE**
(Online, by phone, in person, or by mail.)
or
• **CONTEST THIS VIOLATION**
(By mail or in person, but not both)

(See the reverse side for additional instructions)

ROSENTHAL,JASON

CHICAGO, IL

ldldlllllldllllldlllllllllllllldlllldldl

NOTICE DATE: 11/02/00

VIOLATION NOTICE NO.	DATE AND TIME OF VIOLATION	LOCATION MAKE.PLATE.EXP.	VIOLATION CODE AND DESCRIPTION	FINE AMOUNT
9045105311	10/06/00 09:45	663 W DIVERSEY PLYM 0801	0964190A EXP. METER NON-CENTRAL BUSINESS DISTRICT	$30.00

TO ENSURE PROPER POSTING OF YOUR PAYMENT, PLEASE INCLUDE ALL PAYMENT STUBS FROM THE ENCLOSED PAGES.

WARNING:

If you accumulate 5 or more Final Determinations of parking/compliance liability, any vehicle you own can be booted and impounded until all fines and penalties are paid. **After 10 Final Determinations of parking liability, the City will send certification to the Secretary of State that you are eligible for driver's license suspension.** A Final Determination may be enforced in the same manner as a judgment entered by a court of competent jurisdiction. Final Determinations are collectable by means including collection agency and credit bureau action, and the imposition of liens on real estate and personal estates.

You may now pay online using the web at <www.cityofchicago.org>. If you choose to pay by mail, however, retain the top portion of this Notice for your records and return all stubs in the return envelope provided.

Notice of Violation Stub
You may choose a different option for each Violation Notice. Check a box if you want the same option for all violations listed above, or list each violation number after the option you have chosen for it. Remember to mark all your choices on the return envelope as well.

PAYMENT ENCLOSED FOR VIOLATION NOTICE NUMBERS: ☐ ALL VIOLATIONS ON THIS NOTICE

CONTEST BY MAIL FOR VIOLATION NOTICE NUMBERS: ☐ ALL VIOLATIONS ON THIS NOTICE

REQUEST HEARING FOR VIOLATION NOTICE NUMBERS: ☐ ALL VIOLATIONS ON THIS NOTICE
To The Registered Owner or Lessee of: PAS C367841 IL (LIST VIOLATION NOTICE NUMBERS HERE)

ROSENTHAL,JASON

CHICAGO, IL 60657-1322
TO PAY BY CREDIT CARD FILL IN THE INFORMATION BELOW. THIS PAYMENT WILL NOT BE PROCESSED IF NOT SIGNED.

Card No. ☐☐☐☐☐☐☐☐☐☐☐☐☐☐☐☐☐☐☐☐   Exp. Date ☐☐ — ☐☐

Signature:_____

TOTAL AMOUNT DUE For Violations Listed on This Notice
$30.00
REFLECTS PAYMENTS AS OF:
10/29/00
Please make check or money order payable to the City of Chicago **DO NOT SEND CASH** **1 of 1** TO ENSURE PROPER CREDIT PLEASE RETURN THIS STUB WITH YOUR PAYMENT PLEASE DO NOT FOLD
Amount Enclosed

0904510531140300000000000000000000000000000000000000000000000000000000000000000000000

Contest Parking Ticket on Grounds of Karma *(continued)*

WITHIN <u>7 DAYS</u> OF THIS NOTICE YOU MUST EITHER
PAY THE FINE
(By mail or in person)
or
CONTEST THIS VIOLATION NOTICE
(By mail or in person, but not both)

Remember: By ordinance there are only 7 grounds for contesting a Violation Notice:
1. The cited vehicle or license plate was stolen at the time the Violation Notice was issued.
2. The parking meter was broken or malfunctioning through no fault of your own.
3. The signs regulating parking were missing or obscured.
4. The facts alleged in the Violation Notice contain inconsistent or inaccurate information, or the facts fail to establish that the violation occurred.
5. You were not the registered owner or lessee of the cited vehicle at the time the Violation Notice was issued.
6. The illegal condition described in the compliance violation did not exist at the time the Violation Notice was issued.
7. The compliance violation has been corrected prior to the hearing; provided, however that this defense shall not apply to section 9-64-125; 9-76-140(a); 9-76-160(a),(f); and 9-76-220.

IF YOU FAIL TO RESPOND TO THIS VIOLATION NOTICE, A DETERMINATION OF LIABILITY MAY BE ENTERED AGAINST YOU. If the fine is not paid within 21 days after a Determination of Liability, **a late payment penalty equal in amount to the fine will be added. The determination will become final for purposes of administrative and judicial review.**

9905

If you accumulate 5 or more Final Determinations of parking/compliance liability, any vehicle you own can be booted and impounded until all fines and penalties are paid. **After 10 Final Determinations of parking liability, the City will send certification to the Secretary of State that you are eligible for driver's license suspension.** A Final Determination may be enforced in the same manner as a judgment entered by a court of competent jurisdiction. Final Determinations are collectable by means including collection agency and credit bureau action, and the imposition of liens on real estate and personal estates.

All notices will be mailed to the address of the registered owner as recorded with the Secretary of State.
Payment of the fine and any applicable penalty operates as final disposition of the violation.

TO PAY BY MAIL, check the Payment Enclosed box below and on the envelope. Mail this Violation Notice along with a check or money order payable to the City of Chicago in the orange envelope. **DO NOT SEND CASH.**

TO PAY IN PERSON, bring this Violation Notice to any location listed below on the stub.

TO PAY BY PHONE, CALL (312) 744-PARK (7275) and use either Visa, MasterCard, Discover, Diners Club, or American Express.

TO CONTEST BY MAIL, check the **Contest by Mail** box below and on the envelope. Fill out your name, address, and daytime phone number below. Send this Violation Notice in the orange envelope along with a signed statement setting forth facts that establish a defense. Enclose COPIES of any documents (e.g., photographs, a police report, or your car registration) necessary to show that you are not liable. INCLUDE THE VIOLATION NOTICE NUMBER ON ALL SUPPORTING DOCUMENTS. DO NOT SEND ORIGINALS. THEY WILL NOT BE RETURNED. A decision will be mailed to you.

TO CONTEST IN PERSON before a hearing officer, check the **Request For Hearing** box below and on the envelope, and fill out your name, address and daytime phone number below. Mail this Violation Notice in the orange envelope. You will be notified by postcard of your hearing date.

REMEMBER: YOU MUST MARK THE BOX OF YOUR CHOICE HERE AND ON THE ENVELOPE.

☐ PAYMENT ENCLOSED ☒ CONTEST BY MAIL ☐ REQUEST FOR IN-PERSON HEARING

(Please print your name, address and daytime phone number.)

Amy Krouse Rosenthal

Chicago, IL

If you want to pay in person or drop off the orange envelope, come to:

(West)	**(South)**	**(North)**	**(Central Hearing Facility)**
800 N. Kedzie	2006 E. 95th St.	2550 W. Addison	400 W. Superior
Payments & Inquiries:	Payments & Inquiries:	Payments & Inquiries:	1st Floor
8AM-5PM (M)	8AM-5PM (M)	8AM-5PM (M)	Hours:
8AM-6:30PM (TU-F)	8AM-6:30PM (TU-F)	8AM-6:30PM (TU-F)	8AM-5PM (M)
8AM-3:30PM (SAT.)	8AM-3:30PM (SAT.)	8AM-3:30PM (SAT.)	8AM-6:30PM (TU-F)
Hearing Hours:	Hearing Hours:	Hearing Hours:	8AM-3:30PM (SAT.)
8AM-4PM (M-F)	8AM-4PM (M-F)	8AM-4PM (M-F)	Hearing Hours:
			9AM-4PM (M-F)
			Boot Hearings:
			9AM-3PM (SAT.)

(City Hall)
121 N. LaSalle
Room 107
Payment & Inquiries Only:
8AM-5PM (M-F)

(312) 744-PARK (7275)
Area Codes (217), (309), (618) and (815) call 1-800-336-2446

Contest Parking Ticket on Grounds of Karma *(continued)*

RE: PARKING TICKET

Dear City of Chicago/Department of Revenue, and Police Officer S. Weathers:

I know you say there are only 7 grounds for contesting a Violation Notice, but I just want to be honest with you and see if the following might also be considered a "temporary 8th ground."

On Friday October 6th, 2000, I went to the *Barnes and Noble* on Diversey. I was there before the store even opened. Another gentlemen and myself were there waiting for them to open the doors at 9 am, but I didn't get his name. Anyway, I went to buy books to give as gifts, as we had many occasions coming up that called for a gift.

SO I BOUGHT:
1. A book to take to my friend Ava's house because they had invited us to dinner that night.
2. A book to bring to my friend Kay's cocktail party, which was the next night (Saturday).
3. A book for my friend Susie's birthday (which was that day).
4. A book that I knew my friend Lindy wanted, and I was going to see her later in the day.
5. A book about being sad when you lose your balloon in the sky for my 3-year-old nephew Andrew who had recently lost his balloon. He's OK now.
6. Four magazines for my husband Jason, who had just had knee surgery (torn medial meniscus) that morning, and who therefore would be spending the weekend in bed. His doctor is named Dr. Heffern. He's listed.

I did buy a cup of coffee at the Starbucks café inside-- I felt I deserved that--but besides that, the rest of my purchases were for other people. I rushed around best I could inside and thought I could get everything in less than an hour. Bottom line: I misjudged the amount of time it would take. But in light of the reason for my visit, and that I was only a couple minutes past the expired time, I was wondering if you could extend to me a small break, like a good karma kind of thing.

I am enclosing a check for the 25 cents I should have put in the meter in the first place, and hope we can all call it a day.

Thank you for your time and consideration,

Amy K.R.

Amy Krouse Rosenthal

Enclosures:
photos
petition

169

PETITION

I, the undersigned, say that Amy Krouse Rosenthal is being honest and you should give her a small break.

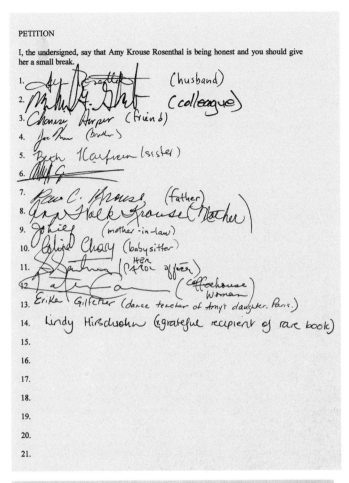

1. ~~~~~~~~~~~~~~~~~~~~ (husband)
2. ~~~~~~~~~~~~~~~~~~~~ (colleague)
3. Chanie Harper (friend)
4. Joe Krouse (Brother)
5. Beth Karfiem (sister)
6. ~~~~~~~~~~~~~~~~~~~~
7. Paul C. Krouse (father)
8. ~~~~ Falk Krouse (Mother)
9. Johie ~~~~ (mother-in-law)
10. Carina Chary (babysitter)
11. ~~~~~~~~~~ (her parole officer)
12. ~~~~~~~~~~~~~~~~ (coffeehouse woman)
13. Erika Gilcher (dance teacher of Amy's daughter, Paris.)
14. Lindy Hirschohn (grateful recipient of rare book)
15.
16.
17.
18.
19.
20.
21.

AMY ROSENTHAL   1939

Date Nov. 6, 2000

Pay to the order of   City of Chicago $ .25

Twenty five cents and zero   Dollars

BANK ONE.
Bank One, NA
Chicago, Illinois 50670

For parking meter   Amy

Contest Parking Ticket on Grounds of Karma *(continued)*

IN THE CITY OF CHICAGO, ILLINOIS
DEPARTMENT OF ADMINISTRATIVE HEARINGS

CITY OF CHICAGO, a Municipal Corporation,
Petitioner.
v.

Ticket: 9045105311
Plate: C367841

Rosenthal,Jason

Chicago IL
Respondent.

FINDINGS, DECISIONS & ORDERS

On 10/06/2000 you were issued a ticket for:

0964190A   EXP. METER NON-CENTRAL BUSINESS DISTRICT

As a defense to this ticket you have asserted that the meter was inoperable
or malfunctioned through no fault of yours at the time the violation was
issued. An Administrative Law Officer has reviewed all the evidence submitted
either in person or by mail, by the City of Chicago and you.

It is the finding of the Administrative Law Officer that the information
supports a determination that the meter was inoperable through no fault of yours
on the date of the violation.

Consequently, you are not responsible for the fine.

ENTERED: AUDREY WADE   078 03/06/2001
              Administrative Law Officer - #   Date

*This order may be appealed to the Circuit Court of Cook County
(Daley Center 6th fl.) within thirty-five days of the order date.

Form letter, but I got off!

Contest Parking Ticket on Grounds of Karma *(continued)*

Pastries

Pastries do not tempt me.

Pay Phone, Guy on

At the convenience store, I couldn't help but overhear a guy having a heated discussion on the pay phone. Over and over he was saying, *It's not my baby. I swear on my mama's life, it's not my baby. You gotta believe me. I swear on my mama's life.* He was in the middle of the store, broadcasting this.

Pedestrian

When I'm about to cross a street and a car stops to let me go, I don't just walk—I sort of jog-dodge across to, you know, show the driver that I'm not taking advantage of this situation. *Yes, I, the pedestrian, have the right of way, but see, I care about you, too, here, just a sec, I'll cross quickly and get out of your way.*

Peppers

Green and red peppers taste less alike than one would think.

Period

I've been getting my period once a month for about twenty-three years now—that's what? 276 times (minus three pregnancies)—and yet I never instantly recognize the slight discomfort in my lower belly and groin as the like-clockwork symptoms of it coming on. I'll think, *I feel a little blechy, what's that vague tweaking sensation?* as I'm putting the breakfast dishes in the sink.

Then later, *Oh, right, I'm getting my period.* There is a science to a woman's cycle—it is not free-form, it is not random—yet I receive it in the same way I receive the weather: simply as it comes, without consulting any charts or forecasts. Just as I know many people carry the precautionary umbrella and can tell you what weather is expected over the weekend, I know many women are actually able to answer the nurse when she asks, *what was the first day of your last period?* While this is a fairly straightforward question, and seems like a reasonable thing to know about oneself, it feels as ludicrous as asking if I wouldn't mind looking at the calendar and telling her when was the last time I tweezed my eyebrows.

PHONE

It's embarrassing when you're getting off the phone and in the rush of going through the in-closing finalities you combine your *take care* with *bye bye* and say *bake care!*

PHONE, GETTING TO KNOW SOMEONE ON THE

When I get to know someone fairly well over the phone, and then, after a while, meet them in person, I am invariably disappointed. It has nothing to do with how attractive the person turns out to be; it has to do with how . . . *human* they turn out to be. When we were speaking on the phone, I envisioned not a distinct person with a face and body, but rather a vague, faceless essence, as if their whole personality manifested itself into an aura that wasn't exactly physical as we know it. So when we met, it was startling to see that they indeed had eyes and torsos and chins. As soon as we went back to communicating by phone, my mind would revert to the (preferred) floaty-aura-portrait.

Photos, Old

It's a powerful thing, coming across an old photo of someone close to you. It makes you pause—

You have to closely examine it. Like a portrait of my grandmother from forty years ago—so vibrant, poised, that nice tweed skirt. Without the mask of old age, her features are more pronounced; she's herself, but crisper. I have a snapshot of my parents from their courtship period, swinging at a park, all smiles and good skin. There they exist as a young man and a teenage woman who love each other, nothing more yet; they are not parents, they have no affiliation to an unborn me. I know how the story unfolds from there—quite happily actually—but in that photo, they are ripe, on the verge, unencumbered, and so very beautiful. I know my own children will one day come across an old photo of me and Jason. *Look at Mom and Dad. They were so young. Look at Mom's hair. And how handsome Dad was.*

Picnic

When you go on a picnic, it is customary to pack three times as much food as you would normally eat. For lunch at home, you'll have a sandwich, chips, maybe a pickle, and be quite satisfied. The picnic version, on the other hand, would be something along the lines of: sandwich, chips (for ten), some Goldfish crackers, pickles, fruit, potato salad and/or coleslaw, a few fried chicken legs, some random leftover from the fridge, and a bag of Tootsie Rolls. Even the napkin ratio is askew: At home, one napkin is standard, but for the picnic you figure about seven per person.

See also: Customary, Things That Are

PIE

There are few gestures kinder than a friend baking you a pie.

See also: Woman Across the Hall

PIÑATA

It would be cool to hang a piñata in the living room and leave it there for a year, looming as a symbol of possibility and sweetness—all the anticipation. A character in a Lorrie Moore story did this. I want to do that one year. Surprise my family. Fill it with something that won't spoil, like Twinkies—yes, a piñata full of Twinkies. Or dozens of CDs—just go wild on CDNow, get a ton of great new music, and then have to wait a year to listen to it. Or I could take it in a totally different direction: fill it with those Styrofoam packing curls, as an antimaterialistic statement about anticipation—*Ah, now see, wasn't the anticipation grander than the actual thing?*—and also because the curls look like the ~ above the *n* in piñata.

PITCHER

At a local pizza place, I overheard a woman ask if she could order one pitcher of soda, but get two separate half pitchers— a half pitcher of Coke and a half pitcher of 7-Up—for the same one-pitcher price. By the look on the bartender's face, I could tell that this was a first. I found the request to be peculiar as well, but also rather brazen and creative.

Survey: For the price of one pitcher, could you get a half pitcher of Coke and a half pitcher of 7-Up?

CHICAGO PIZZA PLACE	RESPONSE
Pizzeria Uno	Would only charge for one.

Pizzeria Due	Would only charge for one.
Gino's on Rush	Would make you order two.
Lou Malnatti's	Would only charge for one.
D'Agostino's	Would make you order two.

PLOT OF SOIL

We have a small plot of soil in our otherwise plant-and-sod-filled backyard. It was asked whether or not we'd like to put some flowers or bushes there. Immediately, reflexively, I said no. Why was I drawn to this empty space of black nothingness? Because it is a relief to me; it is one less thing I have to take care of, to tend to. To look at it is to catch my breath.

POTATO CHIPS

When I eat potato chips, particularly the crunchy kettle kind, I find myself looking through the bag for the *good* chips. Somehow a good chip is one that is extra thick looking, and curled onto itself or folded, as opposed to straight and flat. It is a treat, a victory, to find a really good chip and pluck it from the bag. The thinner, straight, or broken ones aren't nearly as pleasing.

PRIEST

I was at the coffeehouse and debated whether or not to take my backpack (with wallet) into the bathroom with me. I noticed a priest a couple tables away, so I left it.

See also: Wallet, Stolen

PRISON ESCAPE MOVIES

I love prison escape movies: watching the plan unfold; seeing how they sneak each other things when they're out walking in the prison yard; watching them make tools out of spoons and gum wrappers and pen caps; tricking the guards with a dummy body in the bed. They can't make enough of these movies as far as I'm concerned.

PROFOUND

There appears to be a string of seemingly profound messages that have grabbed me along the way. The messages may differ in form—aphorism, quote, song lyric—but what they all have in common is that each promoted an embracing view of life; each elicited an immediate *yes!* feeling in me, which I in turn felt impelled to share with others; each ultimately lost its juice; and each new crush made me feel embarrassed that its simplistic predecessor had actually felt so deep. I believe the first up in the parade was a charm necklace I received when I was about thirteen. It read *live love laugh*. I liked the cadence, the three one-syllable *L* words, but mostly the terse, wise command. *What more is there?* I thought. *Live, love, laugh—that's it.* The next one I can remember presented itself to me when I was twenty, during a summer internship at the ad agency Ogilvy & Mather in New York. I was doing grunt work in the research department. I cannot recall the specifics, but what is vivid is this: There was a passage in a packet I was given, no more than a paragraph or two in length, which jumped out at me and aroused a feeling of *This is what life's about, we have to tell people, this is the perfect thing to base an advertising campaign around!* I highlighted it, attached an emphatic note, and then placed it on my boss's chair. I was sure that I had saved the day, that I had unearthed some incredibly valuable insight that would have numerous reverberations around the office. When it went unmentioned for a day, then two, then a week, I came to terms with my miscalculation, and felt red-faced and small, tricked by my own naive, impressionable self. And it goes on. Mid-twenties I was infatuated with Kierkegaard's "Life must be lived forwards, but can only be understood backwards." Age twenty-eight, doing freelance copywriting for Adidas. Listening to the Indigo Girls' song *Watershed*. With sudden clarity, I was positive that the chorus was anthem material, and I was jazzed by the idea of imparting this message via a running-shoe commercial. *When you're learning to face the path at your pace every choice is worth your while.* My grandiose mission was squelched by a polite *Okay, uh-huh.* And today, at this marker on my existential grid, my philosophical and spiritual capacities intersect in such a way that I am a prime target for—and unabashedly moved by—this Pueblo verse:

> *Hold on to what is good, even if it is a handful of earth.*
> *Hold on to what you believe, even if it is a tree which stands alone.*
> *Hold on to what you must do, even if it is a long way from here.*

PURPLE FLOWER

There is a single purple flower a couple feet from where I am sitting. I am feeling poorly dressed and missing my long hair. I am at Café De Lucca in Bucktown, and there is a purple flower—that's how I would define this moment. And you, your moment? Where are you at this moment? E-mail me and tell me. If you are the hundredth person to do so, I will bake you a pie and FedEx it to you. You will have to trust me on this.

Q-Tip

Inserting a Q-Tip deep into your ear is a great, undiscussed pleasure.

See also: French Fries

R

RADIO, SONG ON

When I'm trying to find something to listen to on the radio, and I come to a song I can't quite decide on—say, a certain Elton John tune—I quickly, subconsciously, check to see what station is playing it. If it's on 93.1—WXRT, Chicago's coolest-without-trying station for as long as I can remember—the song is in my mind *vouched for* and sounds better, it has a certain sparkle. *Bouncer: You with WXRT? Come on in.* Conversely, if I see the call number is 93.9 *(Turn on the Lite, the Lite FM)*, the song's worth and appeal are instantly and drastically diminished merely by its being affiliated with that which feels humdrum and lusterless, and I move on.

RAIN, READING A FAX AND WALKING IN THE

The girl was walking in the rain, reading a fax. The fax had just come in and she was eager to read it. The fax was quickly becoming wet and flimsy. The girl knew she should just wait the ninety seconds until she got to the coffeehouse, where she could read it without the threat of it becoming a soggy, illegible mess. Instead, she kept reading as she walked. It was a good fax, interesting, exciting even. She thought, *This might be the fax that changes things somehow. I might always remember this moment in the rain, reading this fax, knowing that this was the exact minute when I realized something powerful had just happened.* Then she thought, *I am being overly romantic and dramatic. I want this moment to mean something, I am putting all this into the moment, I have concocted something out of nothing because it is raining and the fax is getting wet. It is a highly visual moment, yes. But perhaps nothing more.*

See also: Meaning

RAINBOWS

If rainbows did not exist and someone said *wouldn't it be cool to paint enormous stripes of color across the sky,* you'd say *yes, that would be very cool—impossible, but very cool.* Children are totally tuned in to the miracle of rainbows—that's why they are forever drawing them. There's even something divine about spotting a tiny rainbow in a puddle of water or a splotch of gasoline. *Oh, look! A rainbow!* It would be nice to have some universal ritual connected with rainbows, along the lines of stray penny equals good luck, and car with one headlight equals, say, piddiddle/make a wish. Maybe: See a rainbow, eat a sugar cube. Or see a rainbow, put a dollar in a jar; then when you leave home at eighteen, your mother sends you off with your rainbow money. A friend once told me a story about how he was going through his five-year-old son's backpack and he found a picture of a little boy standing under a rainbow crying. His first thought was, *Oh God, my son is having some serious problems.* When he asked his son about the picture, he told him that he had been playing at school and he saw a rainbow and it was so beautiful that it made him cry.

RAINY DAY

A rainy day comes as a relief. Rain is your pass to stay inside, to retreat. It's cozy and safe, hanging out on this side of the gray. But then the sun comes out in the afternoon, and there's disappointment, even fear, because the world will now resume, and it expects your participation. People will get dressed and leave their houses and go places and do things. Stepping out into the big, whirling, jarringly sunny world—a world that just a few minutes ago was so confined and still and soft and understated, and refreshingly gloomy—seems overwhelming.

Rearranged Furniture

There's the buzz you get the first few times you walk into a room after you've just rearranged some furniture. *Oh, yeah, the couch is over there now, next to the plant . . . and the chairs are here. This is great!* You linger in the doorway and admire it for a few moments, savoring its exciting freshness (it will be two or three days before you're accustomed to it), remembering how it used to be, and how this setup is so much better.

Red Gingham Tablecloth

Certain vestiges from your childhood have a sort of holy status, even if they're the most ordinary of items. For example, at my parents' house, I am comforted instantly by the sight of our red gingham tablecloth, or the pair of large yellow scissors, or even this one certain pan.

Rejection

If I'm looking for a parking spot and I mouth to the person who's sitting in their car, *you leaving?* and he vehemently shakes his head no, I take this as a personal rejection.

Retrieving Messages

The phone rings. I answer it. It's Jason. He was calling to get the messages from the answering machine. I say call back, I won't pick up. We hang up. The phone rings, I answer it. *I forgot!*

I forgot! I say when I hear his voice. We hang up again. The phone rings. I almost, but don't, answer it.

RETURN CALL

If you do not call back, for a brief time I will think nothing of it. But soon I will wonder. Then I will become frustrated. I will toy with the idea of calling you again—perhaps you did not get the message. I will try to refrain from making this second call, retain my pride. I will feel angry every time I retrieve my messages without finding one from you. I will imagine I am not in your good graces, or that I am thought a fool by you, or that you are indifferent to me. I will feel blue. And then eventually I will forget about the whole thing. You will then call back, saying you just got back, you were out of town.

See also: St. John's Wort

RETURNING FROM JOURNEY

We are back from France. I am here, yes, but *there* has not yet lost its hold on me. Baguettes and beaded ankle bracelets and light blue shutters don't yet feel six time zones and an ocean away. It's really something, to return home after a month away. It would seem that the world should have changed in some way, as if to say, out of courtesy, *We understand your journey was illuminating and significant, and because it affected you so, the universe, too, is making a slight but noticeable shift: Chairs will now have five legs, people will walk sideways, and raindrops will be seven percent larger and pinkish in color.* Alas, no welcome-home motorcades, no new shades of rain. But then again, is it not enough that I had the experience, and that the neighbor's dog has learned to fly?

Returning to Life After Being Dead

When I am feeling dreary, annoyed, and generally unimpressed by life, I imagine what it would be like to come back to this world for just a day after having been dead. I imagine how sentimental I would feel about the very things I once found stupid, hateful, or mundane. *Oh, there's a light switch! I haven't seen a light switch in so long! I didn't realize how much I missed light switches! Oh! Oh! And look—the stairs up to our front porch are still completely cracked! Hello, cracks! Let me get a good look at you. And there's my neighbor, standing there, fantastically alive, just the same, still punctuating her sentences with* you know what I'm saying? *Why did that used to bother me? It's so . . . endearing.*

Right Foot

When Paris was little she would ask me, *Mommy, is this shoe on the right foot?* and I would glance over and say, *Yes, Paris, that's the right foot.* But then, a few seconds later, she would ask about the other shoe, *and is this the right foot?* as if there were another option. Depending on my mood, it would be either really irritating or really charming.

Rocket Scientist

If someone tells you he's a rocket scientist or a brain surgeon, you naturally think he's being sarcastic. *A rocket scientist, ha-ha.* It will take you a moment to correctly read his expression and realize, *Oh, wow, he's serious, he really is a rocket scientist, how cool, how . . . weird.*

ROSENDAL

Every time I go to my neighborhood cleaners, the owner, a friendly Chinese fellow, greets me with a loud, staccato "Rosendal!" Not Amy, not Amy Rosenthal / Rosendal, just *Rosendal.* I was wondering why this always makes me feel good, this odd but enthusiastic greeting. And leaving there the other morning it hit me: It reminds me that I am part of a team, a unit, a small urban tribe of Rosendal. It downplays, in a very refreshing way, my individuality and ego and Amy-ness, and instead emphasizes the five-member pack I'm a part of. We're the Rosendals, the mighty, mighty Rosendals. Go, team.

See also: Dry Cleaners

Dry cleaning ticket.

RUNNING INTO SOMEONE

You run into someone you know and stop to chat. Then someone else you sort of know comes along and stops to say hi as well. It turns out that this second person knows the first person you were talking to. The second person says to you, *How do you guys know each other?* You briefly explain, oh, we used to work together, or our kids go to school together, whatever. Turns out the first and second person are pretty good friends. You then have to leave, so you say good-bye to them both. As you walk away, you fantasize/hope that they will turn to each other and remark on what a fine person you are, isn't it funny that they both know you, and then continue for some minutes exchanging flattering tidbits about you.

S

Safire, William

I look at William Safire's *On Language* column in the Sunday *New York Times Magazine* every week and think, *I should read this, this is about the English language, this is relevant and smart and useful, and I do like words.* And then I turn the page.

Sampras, Pete

Jason relayed to me that someone on the train told him he looked like Pete Sampras, and that he responded, *Well, I wish I had his income!* In the retelling of this to me, he said the *well, I wish I had his income* part in a self-mocking way, shaking his head and shoulders ever so slightly, altering his voice, making it lower and kind of singsongy. Standing there at the kitchen counter, I knew we were both totally visualizing the scene, him retorting with that *well, I wish I had his income* doozy. Jason and I presume we are the kind of people who are above those kind of prosaic comments, who understand that it is a completely pedestrian thing to say, and yet there he was, saying it. We laughed about it for several minutes, really, really laughed— so hard, in fact, that I was conscious of my face distorting. And just when we stopped laughing about it, we started again.

Sandwiches

I love but am very particular about sandwiches. I dislike pumpernickel. I dislike thick, doughy bread, such as focaccia and sourdough. Pepperidge Farm Very Thin Bread is my ideal. The sandwich must have mayonnaise. I like and fully appreciate a well-put-together gourmet sandwich, but I also love the sandwiches at gas stations, tightly wrapped in cellophane, with the wilted lettuce.

SANDWICH IN TRASH

A friend told me that a former colleague of ours was retiring, and that there had just been a big farewell party for him. As he told me this, all I could think about was the time I realized that he (the retired fellow) took a half-eaten tuna sandwich out of my garbage can at work and ate it. This was like six years ago  or something, and he was a nice enough guy, yet the one and only identity imprint I've retained is this image of him salvaging and eating the thrown-out sandwich. I recall feeling both grossed-out and incredulous. It was revolting, sure, but he ate it with zero self-consciousness or detectable shame/meekness. He didn't but just as easily could have patted me on the back and said, *"Man. Great stuff you got in your wastebasket, Amy."* I hung up the phone with my friend and realized that this unfortunate recycled-tuna episode was fossilized in my brain like a leaf in stone.

SATURDAY NIGHT LIVE

I'm riveted watching the ending of *Saturday Night Live*. The guest host thanks the cast, says how great it's been working together for the week, then they all wave good-bye and start chatting, mingling. They're up there for a good thirty seconds or so, as the closing theme song plays, and it's certainly in their best interest to appear happy and sociable and generally un-awkward like, but I would think they must be miserably self-conscious. I watch closely to see who's chatting up the host, who is sought after, who looks left out just standing there waving and looking for someone to talk to. I would like to ask them if they dread this whole routine, or if they're fine with it.

See also: Clapping

SENSITIVE

I was having a nice chat with Justin about being sensitive—he had been feeling bad for a friend, and it was really throwing him. *What does sensitive mean exactly?* he asked, and I tried to explain it to him as best I could: *Let's say you see someone crying, and you don't even know them, but you kind of catch their sadness, it somehow jumped into your heart, and this makes you understand a bit how they feel. Or it can work the other*  *way—someone says to you, hey, Justin, nice hat, and they mean it in a fun, teasing, playful way, but you suddenly feel wilted, you can't seem to laugh it off, that's also being sensitive.* I was telling him that he had always been tremendously empathic and sensitive. A moment later I put on my new Christine Lavin CD and it started skipping, over and over, on the word *sensitive. Sensitive. Sensitive. Sensitive.* I turned it off, pressed Play again, and the skipping was gone.

SERVICE CALL

Carolyn speaking, may I help you?
Can I speak with Phyllis?
Do you know her last name?
No, I don't, Carolyn. But now I know I better get your last name in case I have to call back again.
I'm sorry, we don't give out last names.

See also: Depressing, Things That I Find

Sexy

Jason looks especially sexy when he takes off his suit jacket, rolls up the sleeves of his dress shirt, loosens his tie, and plays Pig with the kids.

Shameful

My mind has drifted onto self-involved matters at more than one funeral.

Shopping Center

I will go anywhere with you except the shopping center.

Table

COMPARISONS BETWEEN THE CHURCH AND THE MALL, TWO MODERN PLACES OF WORSHIP

Confessionals = Dressing rooms

Strive to become a better person = Free makeover

Sermons = Shoplifters will be prosecuted

Closer to God = Escalators

Lifelong friends = Gift with purchase of $40 or more

Hallelujah = Sale

Shortcut Through Alley

Jason walks to the El every morning, which is only a few blocks from our house. Occasionally I'll go downtown with him. On one such morning he said, *I've figured out that if I cut through this alley, I save a good thirty seconds.* So through the alley we went. A couple months later we left the house together again. When we got to the alley, I started to turn off but stopped when I noticed he was going straight. *What about the shortcut you showed me?* I asked. *Oh, yeah, I don't use it anymore. I realized life's too short to be walking through alleys past Dumpsters. This way's nicer—this way you can have trees.*

SHOWER TILES

The tiles in my shower have swirly, haphazard designs. Each one is different, and, as with clouds, you can see things in them. One looks just like Ronald Reagan.

SIGN AT 7-ELEVEN

I saw a poster advertising CELEBRITY IMPORTED HAM. How perfect. Indeed, a celebrity is often just that: an imported ham. *Los Angeles, California . . . the land of imported hams.*

See also: Amy Rosenthal; Encyclopedia Spine; Wordplays

SIGN, BATHROOM

I saw a sign in a public restroom that said PLEASE DO NOT FLUSH EXCESSIVE AMOUNTS OF TOILET PAPER OR SHOES DOWN THE TOILET. THANK YOU. I so want to meet the person who flushed a shoe down the toilet, and made a sign like this necessary.

Sign, Handmade

When I see a handmade sign taped to a cash register like WE WELCOME TIPS! I imagine the employee in the back room writing it out in pen or marker. Did the task make him feel focused, hopeful, and productive? Or, conversely, did he feel despondent, a nagging sense of doom?

Silence

I like to spend the in-between hours in silence. After I drop the kids off at school and before I head out for the day, I will return home to a still house. I will open the blinds, straighten up, merge lists, coordinate schedules, compose e-mails, all within the absence of sound. I do not turn on the TV. I do not turn on the radio. Occasionally I will toy with the idea of putting on a CD, but the feeling passes; during these stretches, nothing ever seems more appealing than the quiet. There's nature quiet—vast silence plus crickets plus weird bird noises plus stream gurgling off to the left somewhere. And there's house quiet—vast silence plus clanking of heating system plus dishwasher switching cycles plus hum of refrigerator. The rest of the day is about chatter, cars, music, noise. But for now, it is power button off.

Sitcom, Three Real People as Vividly Described by My Friend A. Who All Seem Like Characters in a

- ► The paleontologist from Iowa, who also writes haiku
- ► The hunchback dentist
- ► A prick named Howie

Sleep

I love sleeping. I love falling asleep on the couch, in the car, on trains, in the sun. I love getting into bed at night, and whenever possible, sleeping late in the morning. I love beds and covers and quilts and pillows. I just love everything about sleeping.

Slow/Fast

I am a slow reader, and fast eater; I wish it were the other way around.

Small Things

Small things are cute. A minuscule dollhouse chair: cute. Ritz Cracker Ritz Bits: cute. Mini pumpkins, thimbles, puppies, those miniature gift books they sell at the counter: all sickeningly cute. Even a tiny heel piece of French bread could be described as cute. This is why young children—even homely ones—exude a certain cuteness; they're actual people, just smaller.

Smells

Table

FAVORITE SMELLS

My father's forehead.
When my kids wake up from their naps all sweaty.
Fire in the fireplace.
Husband's chest.
Rain.

(continued)

Table (continued)

DISTINCT SMELLS

Newborn baby.
Sex.
New car.
New carpet.
Feet.
Pee after eating asparagus.
Nursing home/old people.
Nair.

SMELLS THAT REMIND ME OF SOMETHING

Crayola crayons = childhood.
Gasoline = getting gas with my mom or dad when I was little.
Lysol = when someone would throw up on carpet in
   grammar school.
Blown-out candle of any kind = cake/birthday parties.
Empty beer cans = high school, and college frat parties.

SMOOTH JAZZ

It would be hard to not let your fondness for smooth jazz come
between us.

See also: Bad Movie

SNEEZING

Jason sneezes. *God bless you,* I say. He sneezes again. *God bless you.*
He sneezes a third time. *Bless you,* I say kinda angrily. He
sneezes for the fourth time. *Stop it already,* I say. *It's annoying now.*
As if he can help it.

Snowflake

If I say *snowflakes on your eyelashes*, you can feel it, can't you? You are there, on the snowy day.

Soup

A good soup attracts chairs. This is an African proverb. I can hear the shuffling and squeaking on the wood floor, the gathering 'round. This, from just five well-chosen words.

Special

I went to pay for my tea and bagel at the coffeehouse and the woman behind the register said, *You know what? It's free today. What, huh, why?* I asked. *Just because,* she replied. *Wow,* I thought. *She intuitively senses I'm special. I bet I'm the only person she's ever given free tea to. She must be picking up on my unique energy; my significance; that I've been brooding and feeling contemplative lately; that I feel like I finally want to read Proust.* The other worker tilted her head and whispered to me, *She does that all the time—to break the monotony, you know?*

See also: Friend You Thought Confided in You;
Humbling; Running into Someone

Spices

I know a woman named Saffron, another woman named Curry, and a horse named Basil.

Spilled Linguine

I spilled a package of linguine on the kitchen floor. My immediate reaction was, *What a bummer, what a waste.* But then: *Wait a second, it's going directly into a pot of boiling water. Sterilizing these noodles and cooking them are one and the same. Cool.*

St. John's Wort

> ### Experiment
>
> #### DAY ONE
>
> I'm not sure if I feel any less blue yet, but I did notice that when I put the *Tarzan* CD on in the car for the kids, I started to sing along.
>
> #### DAY TWO
>
> Forgot to take it.
>
> #### DAY THREE
>
> Bored with experiment.

St. Tropez

Jason and I spent the afternoon in St. Tropez. At the end of the day, we planted ourselves at a café to people-watch. I kept wondering if I would see anyone I knew, despite the fact that we hadn't seen any Americans for two weeks. Nonetheless, I thought about the odds, running into an old college pal or an acquaintance from the health club. I figured surely I had to know *someone* here, even if only remotely. What if an announcement were made over the P.A. system (as if St. Tropez had a citywide P.A. system): *Excuse me, Mesdames et Messieurs, does anyone here know a Ms. Amy Krouse Rosenthal of Chicago, Illinois? If you know or have ever heard of such a person, please report to dock number nine.*

 I think I know an Amy Rosenthal.

 (Pointing to dock) *Elle est là, Monsieur.*

 Amy?

 Steve? Steve Prebish? Is that you?

STARING

It is hard not to.

STATEMENT

There is so much I want to say. Someone has to say it. It's never been said before, and it desperately needs to be articulated. As a statement it is at once powerful yet tender, obvious yet insightful; to finally say it is to release a hundred butterflies. But for now, all that surfaces is an unintelligible burst of consonants set to a drumbeat. It will do.

STRAWBERRIES

While rinsing strawberries, you have the privilege of spotting and eating the very best one, the deep red jewel that is free of indents and blemishes.

STREET FAIR

I'm at the street fair. *This booth looks interesting. And that one across the way with the hats and sundresses. Oh, and back there, I missed the sugar-covered peanuts.* I set out with organized intentions, to walk up one aisle and then calmly, tidily, down the next. But it's no use; I inevitably zag. What I'd prefer, what I suppose I would do if I could, what I suppose this is all about really, is I'd just like to swallow—in all its messy, bursting vibrancy—the whole fair at once.

See also: Completion; Flight Habits; Magazines

Stupid Slow Driver

When I see a really slow driver, I have to pull up alongside him to see what this person looks like, to confirm my suspicions. I am certain I will find a distinctly stupid-looking person. *Ah, yes, he looks totally stupid. Stupid slow driver.*

Sunday

Though this has never materialized, I still think of Sunday as the day when I will stay home and make a large vat of chili for the neighbors, and also boil a sack of potatoes so we can use them in various ways throughout the busy workweek.

See also: Busy; Folded Quilts; Soup; Woman Across the Hall

Sunday *New York Times*

Sunday holds the most promise. It is the day when I will sit down with a cup of coffee and read all the sections of the paper, instead of just the *Magazine,* "Arts and Leisure," and the *Book Review.* Monday comes and I think, *Okay—the paper's still pretty fresh and timely; I'll read it tonight.* Tuesday comes and I have a slightly diluted version of my Monday stance. Wednesday I ignore it. Thursday is the day when I'm like, *Face it, I'm not going to read all of it this week, and besides, a whole new one is coming in four days,* and then I gather up the sections and throw them out.

Sunny Day

I stepped outside. It was bright, very bright, and sunny. There was a long patch of yellow flowers across the street. The flowers were in full bloom, so alertly yellow, as if plugged in. I felt like I was in a Claritin commercial.

SYNCHRONIZATION

Synchronized anything is so cool to watch. Twenty-five dancers moving the exact same way at the exact same time—exhilarating. Same with water ballet/synchronized swimming—the trademark aerial view of those perfect circles they make, the way their legs all come up at the same time, how they disappear under water and then . . . *pop back up!* in unison. Fantastic. Other examples: (1) A marching band. (2) Dolphins at a zoo dolphin show. (3) The flawless choreography of a flock of birds—*dip down, turn to the right, turn to the left,* all while in fluttering formation. (4) Even that mirror game we used to play as kids. Two people face each other. One leads, the other tries to copy his movements, ideally without delay. *Right arm slowly up, then back down, look over your left shoulder, then back . . .* (5) And vineyards. Motionless, yes, but still, row upon row upon synchronized row.

T

TA-DA!

Children get to say *ta-da!*, and I guess magicians, but other than that, it's an underutilized expression. I'm trying to think—an adult might say it as she waltzes in with the turkey, or a homemade cake. But a self-congratulatory *ta-da!* would certainly be warranted for any number of daily accomplishments. I cleaned out the trunk of my car. *Ta-da!* I finished filling out the insurance application. *Ta-da!* I made the bed. *Ta-da!*

TAKING A PICTURE WITH A FRIEND

You're taking a picture with someone. You're standing there all chummy, arm in arm. After the picture's taken, you drop your arms, let your face go back to neutral. But then the person with the camera says, *Oh, one more, just to be sure.* There's an awkward moment where you don't exactly know if you should put your arms around each other again, reenact the camaraderie. The second picture is wrought with self-awareness. *Her hand feels looser on my waist. She's uncomfortable, too. Should I take my hand off her shoulder and put it on her waist?*

TAKING UP SOMETHING NEW

When I take up something new—say knitting, or the Nordic-Track—there's a period of time where I think, *Who knows, this may be just the thing for me. From this point on it will be part of the way people define me.* As in: *Oh yeah, Amy, I know her; she's the one who knits those hats.* It's galvanizing, this new thing, partially because it is fun and interesting, partly because it is simply new, and largely because of the prospect of it becoming an integral part of my life and identity. *I will always have knitting needles with me. I will know all the good knitting stores. I will become an expert on yarn.* While there are things that have stuck since I fell into them (I dye my hair red; I like yoga; I am known for concocting salads and dressings), it seems, in many cases, the new things slip right off me. It's as if their sticking were nearly impossible, that to try to adopt them would put me head to head with my destiny.

Table

THINGS I'VE BEEN INTO (IN CHRONOLOGICAL ORDER)

Passion	What Age(s)	Total # of Years
Coloring, drawing	3–18	15 years
Piano	8–16	8 years
Ziggy	14–20	6 years
Fibonacci numbers	8th grade	1 year
Not eating sweets	18–19	1 year to the day
Tennis	13–23	10 years
Swimming	21–31	10 years
Writing time with *h*, as in *8h15*	20–32	12 years
Not eating meat	23–28	5 years
Advertising writing	21–32	11 years
Green algae nutrition supplement	Two days in my late 20s	N/A

(continued)

Passion	What Age(s)	Total # of Years
Making bracelets out of antique buttons with boyfriend/husband	24–28	4 years
Creating T-shirts with expressions on them, with husband	26–30	4 years
NordicTrack	One week in late 20s	N/A
Running	31–35	4 years
Knitting	Two weeks in late 20s	N/A
Reading biographies about Proust	32–35	3 years
Waking up early on school days before kids to shower and prepare breakfast	One day in mid-30s	N/A
Cooking Friday-night dinners	29–?	TBD
Yoga	36–?	TBD

TALKING WHILE COLORING OR MAKING ART

There is a specific kind of talking that occurs between two people who are engaged in the creation of art. I was aware of this as a kid when I was coloring with a friend, then in drawing classes in college, and again now when I color side by side with Paris. This banter, this *art speak,* is nonsensical, meandering, intimate, and purposeful. It is what keeps reconnecting you to

the other person as you drift/zoom in and out of the micro-
world of your painting, or art project, or coloring book. For a
few minutes there you will all but disappear; you'll actually be
inside your art, walking around a specific five square inches of
your canvas, getting to know the thickness of every black line,
tweaking the blue-green splotch at the bottom, adding a little
triangle in the corner. Then, zap, you're beamed back, and
upon your return you'll say something like *brown, brown, please
pass the brown, brown is the best in town.* But what you are really saying
is, *Hi, I'm still here with you, how you doing, glad we're coloring together.*

Tears

I cry in all the usual places: weddings; the births of babies—my
own, yes, but even those born to strangers on Lamaze videos;
the kids' school shows, when they stand up there on the stage
singing in their one nice shirt they've outgrown; certain com-
mercials, the ones equal parts polished and mushy. I think
some of my biggest cries have been at movies. *Dancer in the Dark*
made me cry so hard for so long that all I could do was put
my drained self to bed and apologize the next morning to a
friend whose party I missed. *The Double Life of Veronique* made
me cry, though I think its magic was later somewhat tarnished
when I heard the 444-FILM guy refer to it as *The Double Life
of Veronica—ka* in place of *ique,* emphasis on the *ron*—in his
overzealous, peculiarly brash manner. As a teenager, *Love Story*
made me cry in the hugest way. Ali MacGraw's beauty. Her
long middle-parted hair. The way they looked together with
their collegiate scarves in the snow. And of course the theme
song didn't help—C E E C C E E C C E F E D D D B B. Years
later I would learn that this movie was what one would call
manipulative, lowbrow, a tearjerker. But it will always be what it was
for me then in the mid-seventies—a great movie that made me
have to take deep breaths and blow my nose.

As a kid, the minute I sensed my parents had sat me down for a *you've disappointed us* discussion, the cry feeling would materialize, reducing me to nothing more than a pulsating throat and two blurry eyes. This kind of admonish-induced cry happens less frequently now that I am an adult, but a few instances do stand out. One was on a trip we took with another family. On the very last night we made a let's-use-up-all-our-groceries dinner together, and prepared everything in the other family's quarters. In the middle of the night I woke up with a start: *The dishes! We left all those dishes, pans, in their sink.* I felt sick thinking about it. First thing the next morning I brought it up—*I'm so sorry, I don't know how that happened, all the wine, I'm so sorry*—thinking my friend would just brush it off—*don't be silly, not a big deal.* But in the nicest possible way she said, *well, I wasn't going to say anything, but yeah, we were pretty ticked; the kids and I stayed up for a while doing them all.* She was totally over it, she said. But that I had done something so thoughtless and sloppy and ungracious— fine, so it wasn't intentional—filled me with such shame and remorse that I broke out in tears. I tried not to; God knows I tried to hold the cry back. But there was no containing it. My crying made her feel worse for having said anything. We hugged, and then soon departed in our separate rental cars. I cried off and on for another thirty minutes as we drove along the dirt country road.

Lately, which is to say in my late thirties, I find that I am often moved to tears in my car, alone, listening to music. The combination of the quiet plus music plus cocoonlike detachment plus open-road reflection seems for me to be a potent mix. *I really love my sisters,* I'll think. *We used to be so little together, with our matching floral parkas and crooked bangs, and now we are grown-ups with families of our own.* Or I'll be excited to share some news with my parents— work-related, or a milestone with one of the kids, or one of those *you're-not-going-to-believe-what-happened* stories. News of any kind doesn't feel real, or thoroughly incorporated somehow, until it's been relayed to them. I'll picture the scenario:

Hi, Mom.

Ames!

Hi. Hey, I want to tell you guys something.

Okay, wait, let me get Dad, he'll want to hear. Paul, pick up the other phone; Amy is on; she wants to tell us something.

Yep, I'm here.

You see? They're just so sweet.

While I'm driving, I often think about Ellen. Ellen lived with us for years, helped looked after me and my younger brother and sisters. When I was twenty-four, she was murdered in her apartment. I got the call when I was at work. Within minutes we were all at my parents' house. What else could we do but cling, and splash water on our red, puffy faces. Ellen wasn't formally educated, but oh, she was smart. She always said she had *mother wit*. She could keep our teenage secrets when it was all right to, but she would also know exactly when to call us on our shit. She would warn us of shady friends. My teenage boyfriend was a good egg and she appreciated this fact in a way that I was only fully able to later in retrospect.

We went to the funeral at her church. There was a lot of singing. My legs felt weak. I was just so sad, stuffed, and sick from a buffet of sadness: heartsick sad, mad sad, numb sad, exhausted sad. It was a long time before anyone could mention her name without me having to excuse myself. A few weeks before she died, I had finally—and how glad was I now—followed through on an idea the two of us had tossed around since I'd moved into my own place. *Come sleep over, Ellen! I'll make you dinner . . . you can see my place . . . I can take you to the train the next morning.* I made her pasta, I remember that. But she didn't like the kind I chose; I should have known better—it was the wrong shape, too unusual, too city-girlish. I should have made rice. We watched Johnny Carson together and she rubbed my back like she used to. I felt guilty about it in a way because I wanted this to be my chance to dote on her, but it felt so nice. I tried to insist on her sleeping in my bed—*no, Ellen, you take the bed, really, please, you are not sleeping on my couch*—but she would have none of it. So there we were—small me in my big bed, big Ellen on my small couch. But she was happy that night, I know she was; me too.

Another person who often comes to mind when I'm driving is Oscar, the man who ran the overnight camp I went to for eight summers. His wife, Natalie, had MS. I never saw her out of her wheelchair. She was withered and shaky, broken and trapped. On a good day she would raise her arm and wave. *H-h-hi, g-g-girls.* This was not all: Their daughter, Renee, who always seemed to be about eighteen to me, had some horrible disease since birth. We didn't know what it was, but she looked a bit off; I mostly remember her fingers looked funny. She was supposed to have died years before, but she kept going and going; everyone knew hers was borrowed time. I spent two months at this camp every summer from the age of nine to the age of sixteen, yet I don't recall ever giving serious thought to these tragic figures. They were just two more camp fixtures: There's the lodge; there's the tetherball pole; there's the lake; there are Natalie and Renee. They are all dead now; I believe Renee went first, then Natalie, then Oscar.

Hi, Oscar.

Amy. What a surprise. How are your sisters?

They're good, thanks. I'm sorry that you died, Oscar, and Natalie and Renee, too.

Yes, we did, didn't we. It was time.

Listen. I want to tell you. I want to tell you that I think about you a lot. It had to have been so hard for you all those years, running a camp, and looking after your sick wife and daughter. I didn't know the word stoic *back then, but that's what you were. I mean, Jesus Christ, Oscar. I'm really sorry. For what you had to go through. And for not realizing more back then, paying closer attention, offering to help or something. You never made us girls feel burdened with your hardship. You carried it all. You gave us everything. I loved camp so much. I still know every camp song. "In the Northwoods of Wisconsin, beneath the skies so blue . . ." You were a good man. I teach things to my kids that you taught me. It must have been painful watching a hundred and fifty healthy girls frolic about, a hundred and fifty pairs of strong legs, a hundred and fifty strong hearts, a hundred and fifty promising futures. We were just oblivious, we were so busy having the god-damn time of our lives.*

Amy, it's okay. You were twelve.

It's not okay.

It's okay.

I wanted to tell you this.

THANKFUL

I'm thankful for my health, my childhood, and spell-check. I'm thankful for our new hot water tank and how we no longer have to coordinate our dishwashing with our bathing. I'm thankful for the wide range of flavors potato chips come in—mesquite barbecue in particular. I'm thankful my job doesn't require wearing panty hose, or a honking red nose. I'm thankful that I have not had to fight in a war. For platform shoes. For coincidences. I'm thankful there are people who know exactly how to build a house—it seems like such an impossible task to me. I'm thankful for all the people who ever left, in those dishes by the cashier, a penny I later used. I'm thankful that I'm done with the phase of my life where I had to spend hours filling in little circles with a number-two pencil. That I don't know everything that people say behind my back. That my husband has zero interest in golf. That I am not a Kennedy. That Hitler wasn't a twin. I'm thankful when plans I made for reasons other than just wanting to fall through. I'm thankful I was born after the advent of indoor plumbing, and after the popularity of corsets. I'm thankful for insect repellent, nonstick pans, and Velcro. I'm thankful for the sun—it just keeps rising, and never asks for anything in return. I'm thankful that people in real life don't spontaneously break into song like they do in musicals, and that some weeds look like flowers, and that at the end of a really bad day there is sleep. I'm thankful for smart, alert air-traffic controllers. For right turn on red. I'm thankful every time I pull up to a parking meter with free time remaining. I'm thankful that a movie, which costs $200 million to make, still costs only nine dollars to see. I'm thankful for *maybe*.

Thanking a Stranger for Taking Your Picture

You're with a group of friends and one of you asks a stranger, *Would you mind taking a picture of us?* The stranger obliges. Afterward, everyone shouts *thanks!* As the thank-yous die down and the stranger starts to walk away, you turn to him, look him in the eye, and say, in a real enunciated and sincere way, *thank you,* like you and the stranger have an understanding, and that everyone else's thank-yous were cute and flippy, but yours was the one that counts.

3841 Bordeaux

3841 Bordeaux was my address for a very long time. Technically, I lived there eleven years—from the age of three to the age of fourteen—but it felt like a hundred and eleven years. For those were the years when a year was an eternity of days. Time was somewhere between stretched-out and nonexistent. Life wasn't forward-moving then; life just *was*. It was as big and beautiful and motionless as my mahogany bedroom dresser. 3841 felt as forever to me then as the finiteness of life feels to me now. One could count on things. Always: curled-up worms on the sidewalk after it rained. Always: the comforting weekend sound of the Cubs game or the Bears game on TV; the rise and fall of the announcer's voice; the muffled roar of the crowd; not understanding any of it; steady, likable background noise. Always: my dad's bottom drawer of neatly folded white undershirts; being able to take them to sleep in, so soft. Always: holidays with the uncles at the card table playing Hearts. Always: reading the cereal box while we ate breakfast, Beth and I. Always: being in my room, hearing the mechanical chinking of the garage door opening and knowing my parents were home. Always: my dad whistling and dressed nicely, even on Sundays, a sweater and pressed slacks. Always: my mom shaving in the tub, one leg hovering in the air, razor gracefully raking from ankle up to knee. Always: getting into bed and feeling the cold underside of the pillow against my forearm. Always: the late-night lullaby of ice knocking against my parents' water glasses as they came upstairs. There were a lot of always's. Even today the number 3841 sounds more like infinity to me than the word *infinity* itself.

TIP OF TONGUE

And then in the middle of the night, thank God, the name comes to you. (Blythe Danner.)

TOAST

I cannot stress this enough: One second your toast is fine, golden brown; the next second it is black.

TOAST, DRAWING GOOD

You can be really bad at something, but because kids cannot do that thing at all, and perhaps have never even seen anybody else do that thing, they think you're really good at it. For example, I drew this at breakfast and Miles said, *Wow, Mom, you draw really good toast.*

Trainer

I would like, just once in my life, to have an opportunity that would require me to work out with a trainer for an entire year, à la Linda Hamilton for *Terminator 2*, or Denzel for *Hurricane*. Though as a writer, I'm not sure how this would ever come about.

Translating a Poem

That they are able to translate a poem that rhymes—from Portuguese to English, let's say—to be able to find just the right word with the right nuance, and have it rhyme with *solicitous* to boot, is just tremendous.

Travel

In the end, no one really wants to hear about your trip.

See also: Other People; Returning from Journey

Tube of Ointment

I could never figure out a good way to open an ointment tube. I would poke the aluminum seal with a kitchen fork prong or with tweezers. I was in my early thirties when I learned that the outside of the cap was designed specifically to puncture it.

Tuesday Night

There are proponents of New Year's Eve, and there are proponents of regular Tuesday nights. I am one of the latter, much happier residing in the wake of the mundane. One evening after a good dinner, the kids and I were taking a walk, and we got stopped by a complete stranger. She had seen us from her window, she said, and ran down because the back of her dress was jammed in the zipper, and she couldn't undo it herself. The kids stood and watched as I helped her unzip her dress. She thanked us and went back inside. That was a really great night.

Such was the case even when I was a schoolgirl: I tended to dread field-trip days, all the excitement while getting our coats and lining up, the singing and bouncing on the bus, the museum exhibits that we were supposed to look at and learn something from, that curious feeling of detachment, and the guilt that I wasn't enjoying it. How wonderfully uneventful the next day was, everything subdued and back to normal, pencil sharpener over there, teacher by the chalkboard, us quietly working away at our desks.

See also: Happiness

U

Uneasy Conversation

In a conversation where I'm slightly nervous, I'll find myself using some random word over and over, a word that I am otherwise not particularly attached to, like with Greg at lunch it was the word *version*. *In the other, better-scripted version of this day, I don't spill vinaigrette on your folder.*

Update

I have started reading, and liking, fiction. This was not the case a year and a half or—not that this book is chronological—99 pages ago. Aside from a handful of short story collections (Carver, Canin, Moore) and an isolated novel here and there, my post-college reading-for-pleasure era has been marked by a shocking absence of fiction. I have been trying to understand how this change came about, how or why the gateway suddenly opened for a nonfiction junkie such as myself.

False starts and stops, that's all it ever was for me with fiction, like when you're in the midst of an intense story on the phone but the other person keeps going *sorry, can you hang on a sec, that's my call waiting, just a sec.* Not very conducive to beginning, middle, climax, and end storytelling. That's how it was with trying to read a novel. My brain would, mid-paragraph, click over to retrieve some other unrelated thought. I couldn't keep it flowing long enough for the all-out-of-the-gate-at-once characters to break from the pack and reveal themselves as individuals whose names conjured up specific traits. Nor could I hang on long enough for the text to begin to read as a story and not just line upon line of random, comma-infested sentences.

My attachment to facts and truth more or less began when I learned to read. From the get-go I was crazy for biographies; there was a series for young readers about legendary women (presidents' wives, Amelia Earhart, etc.) that I couldn't get enough of. I recall, a bit later, being thrown by the idea that something in print might actually not be fact. If the words were printed, they carried so much power. *The authority had spoken,* and it took me awhile to get hip to the don't-believe-everything-you-read adage. My favorite bedtime story for my entire third year of life wasn't a made-up story at all, but rather a series of bullet points outlining the characteristics of our new suburban house and how, unlike in the city, we would have a backyard, and what specifically we were going to be eating there (steak, corn, and soda pop). I would ask my dad to tell me again and again.

After completing an early working draft of this book, I wanted to put it all to the test, to verify, to erase any possibility of troubling cloudy grayness. Who could do this? Matching memories with family or friends wasn't absolute enough: think *Rashomon.* And God had never spoken to me in any clear way, not to mention the difficulty of getting Him a manuscript. There was only one solution I could think of: a polygraph examination. So one afternoon, with wires sticking out of my head and chest, I responded to an administrator's questions. *Is what you've written in this book the truth as you know it?* And (because I was curious): *Did you write this book to the best of your ability?* I was happy when her analysis arrived a couple weeks later saying I'd passed, but by then, strangely, and out of nowhere, I had read a novel from start to finish, loved it, and (I see now in retrospect) had officially been admitted into the kingdom of fiction. This was in December of 2002.

From there, things started unraveling. I became okay with urban myths. I am now able to appreciate them for the stupid little stories that they are, and not agonize over whether or not the girl who had spiders crawl out of her cheek is an actual real girl or a totally made-up not-real girl. Also: I can improvise in the kitchen. Prior to my fiction arousal, I'd have to follow a recipe to the T. The recipe was the truth. You didn't start throwing in cayenne pepper just because you felt like it, or use one tablespoon of sesame oil instead of two. That was fiction. Now if I feel like following the recipe exactly, fine. But I can also deviate and concoct without feeling like I'm doing something wrong.

But still, what then should I attribute this shift to? Was it that I had to fill myself up with a certain amount of facts—nearly forty years' worth—before I was technically ready to appreciate what one could do with facts, how they might be folded in, altered, stretched, and pureed? Was it that, unbeknownst to me at the time, while replacing a roll of paper towels, I was struck with a lightning bolt of literary maturation on, say, the morning of December 21?

I've come up with this explanation: people change. It's as uninteresting as that. People change.

Who am I? Oh, yes: I'm the kind of person who doesn't like fiction, country music, or cilantro. We use these defining truths to help us stay in the lines of ourselves. We think we have to hold on to these labels, we feel comfortable holding on to these labels, but it turns out the labels are removable, you can peel them right off. *Okay then, change of plans: I'm the kind of person who likes nonfiction and fiction, and used to not like cilantro but now likes it, but still doesn't care for country music.*

———

I want to tell you something. And this is 100 percent nonfiction true. I have been struggling with this Update entry for the past several weeks. Today, July 15, 2004, is the last day that I can add anything new to this book before the designers start killing me. Inbetween writing and stressing this morning, I checked my e-mail. I had been trying to track down a fellow who some years ago wrote to tell me that he'd found a copy of a short essay of mine in the trash at our neighborhood Kinko's and enjoyed it, whatever. We had e-mailed back and forth for a while, but eventually went on our merry cyber ways. Themes in that essay turned out to be stepping stones to the conception of this book, and, being a sucker for serendipity and bringing things full circle, I thought it might be interesting to reconnect with him now, but my attempts were in vain. About two hours ago, he turned up in my in-box. At the end of his delightful e-mail he signed off with a quote. It is the most perfect summation of everything I've tried to say on this subject of not liking and now liking fiction: *I have contradicted myself, in order to avoid conforming to my own taste.* So thank you, Marcel Duchamp. And thank you, Jeffrey Rawwin.

V

Van Gogh Prints

I was writing at the coffeehouse when in struts a young guy, twentyish, peddling poorly framed Van Gogh prints. He had a large box of them, dozens of these two-by-three-foot, faux-gold-framed, ready-to-hang posters. They looked awful. To make matters worse, he was rambling on about how if he sold just a few more, he'd be set with beer money for the week. The whole scene was unbearable. This was, after all, Van *Gogh*. *Vincent* van Gogh. *Starry Night* Vincent van Gogh. Truth splendor torment pain pain pain paint Van Gogh. Who now, a century and change later, has emerged on the other side of fame and glory, the side where your work is so universally known and accepted that it turns up on key chains, and hand towels, and prints being hawked door to door by a fellow who's a six-pack away from being passed out on the couch. It seems not even an artist like Vincent van Gogh is exempt from the rule that in time, the sublime is reduced to Cheez Whiz.

Table	
CULTURAL COMING-OF-AGE	
How I always thought it was pronounced	**How the sophisticated apparently pronounce it**
Van Go	Van Gogk
Prowst	Proost
Budapest	Budapesh

W

Wabi-Sabi

I was noticing how more and more I was feeling both happy (actually, content) and sad at the same time. Happiness always seemed to be tinged with sadness, and, strangely, vice versa. I started asking around if anyone knew a word that meant happy and sad at the same time. People offered up *melancholy*, but that wasn't it—that's more sad than happy. And no, it's not *bittersweet,* either. I'm talking about complete happiness and complete sadness simultaneously, the way Van Morrison's music makes you feel, let's say. Maybe it's 55 percent happy, 45 percent sweet/sad. It's the way you feel when you run into a friend from grammar school, someone you haven't seen in twenty years, and it turns out he is no longer nine years old, he's a grown-up telling you about his work, he is a balding, padded stand-in, but it's so fantastic to see him, this generational ally you were shuffled along with from grade to grade, this person who once made up a significant percent of your world because back then your world was only ten miles wide and thirty kids deep, and as you hug good-bye—*it was so great to see you, so amazing, okay you too, take care*—you know that this chance encounter may very well constitute your one and only reunion.

It is feeling content, peaceful, hyper-aware of loss, in awe, perfectly, gently happy/sad. What is the word?

I continued probing friends, even strangers, for a few weeks; eventually I got the hint that no one really felt this way, and anyway, there didn't seem to be a word for it, so I stopped asking/searching.

A couple months later, I picked up *Utne Reader* magazine. I was drawn to the cover story about wabi-something. It reminded me of the word *wasabi*, which I like, so I bought the issue.

Here's what I found:

SABI: *a mood—often expressed through literature—of attentive melancholy.*

WABI: *a cozier, more object-centered aesthetic of less as more.*

WABI-SABI: *As a single idea, wabi-sabi fuses two moods seamlessly: a sigh of slightly bittersweet contentment, awareness of the transience of earthly things, and a resigned pleasure in simple things that bear the marks of that transience.*

This was it. This was exactly it. The word/concept I had been searching for had been there all along, tucked away in twelfth-century Japanese culture, waiting patiently for my straight-ahead gaze to shift a bit eastward.

See also: Lucky

From baby book. "At four years and five months Amy said: 'I am very sad and very happy. I am sad because I miss Grandma. That's why I don't want to grow up because I won't have a grandma. It's not like when you're little. I'm happy because I have so many friends.'"

Waking

When I wake up in the morning, my mind slowly reels in the hard facts that transfer me from subconscious to conscious: *I am in bed. That is my husband's leg. I ate too much dip last night. My neck-lace is still on. I am upset at L. The baby is awake.*

Wallet, Forgotten

I was in the air, on my way to New York, when I realized I'd left my wallet at home. How would I get from the airport to my hotel? I panicked and cried and panicked and cried, and then mustered up the courage to ask the woman next to me if I could borrow some money. (*I'm an honest person—I will pay you back, I promise. I know this is weird, I'm so sorry to bother you.*) She said yes. We got to talking. It turned out she was the mother of a work colleague.

Wallet, Stolen

I was at the local library picking out books with the kids. We were having a good time. I took them to the bathroom with me and put my wallet on top of the toilet-paper dispenser. A minute later, outside the bathroom, I realized I'd left it there. Too late—the wallet was gone. I was surprised; stealing a wallet at a place where people worship books seems like a disconnect, sacrilegious.

Justin, for the first time ever, had decided to bring his new wallet with him that morning. It was a birthday present from his aunt, and it contained two dollars, both of which were from the Tooth Fairy. When I flipped out about my stolen wallet, he said, *It's okay, Mom—you can have mine.*

WEALTHY

I was at the home of an insanely wealthy individual. While standing by his shiny grand piano, it became evident that the thing that separates the insanely wealthy from the rest of us is that the insanely wealthy enlarge all their photographs. That's it right there. Every photo on his mantel and coffee table was an eight-by-ten—not the standard three-by-five, or your occasional five-by-seven—I'm saying, eight-by-ten, across the board. There were dozens of them. There was the *Here I am with the President* eight-by-ten, and the *Here I am with Nelson Mandela* eight-by-ten. But even the requisite *grandkids naked in the back-yard* shots were blown up and thoughtfully framed. The rest of us, on the other hand, make do with our fridge frame magnets; our five-by-seven frames from Target; our flock of cheap, bland frames we seem to have been born with.

WEATHER, ASKING ABOUT THE

At the doctor's office, the receptionist was checking me in and asked, *So, is it still snowing out there?* As if she had been locked up for days. As if she was relying on the arrival of us lucky, no-madic patients to bring her the news of the streets.

WHITE SOCK

A white sock somehow became affixed to our garage door. Every time the garage door went up, so did the little white sock. I began to look forward to watching the sock rise up, and go down; it was an odd, daily, 100 percent cotton beacon of joy. And while I knew the sock would ultimately, inevitably, unattach itself, when that day came, and no sock rose up with the garage door, I was disheartened.

Winking

It takes a lot of confidence to wink at someone.

Woman Across the Hall

I can't remember the name of the eighty-something-year-old woman who lived in the apartment across the hall when I was twenty-three and living in San Francisco. She was so nice. She often left homemade cookies with quaintly formal notes at my door.

Woman at Coffeehouse

I was trying to get some writing done at the coffeehouse. An older woman—maybe she was in her late seventies—asked me what I was working on. This kind of bugged me. First of all, I have trouble with that question—that's my own thing, I know, but I don't know how to answer it without sounding either pretentious (if I try to accurately explain it, really get into it) or ridiculously inarticulate (if I try to give them the gist while keeping it ambiguous). And besides, people don't really want an *answer* answer, they want a categorical answer: Essay. Article. Novel.

With the older woman, I opted for an evasive (conversation-stopping) answer, and immediately felt guilty for not being friendlier, more chatty; clearly, the woman was lonely, for God's sake. So when I got up to go to the bathroom some minutes later, I stopped at her table to say hi. She seized upon this gesture and proceeded to tell me all her ailments. I kept saying, *Oh, that's terrible, I'm so sorry to hear that,* and I was, but all the while I felt insincere and useless. I finally mumbled something about getting back to work, and when the older woman got up to leave later, I didn't even look up.

Word of the Day

I was taking a bath. Paris was about to practice violin, and I said, *Why don't you practice in here, keep me company?* After a few minutes of listening to her I said, *Oh, Paris, it sounds so beautiful in here, the acoustics are perfect.* Then, because the teaching moment seemed too good to pass up, this tangible example of the word *acoustics,* I tried to define it for her. But then I quickly realized, *Who am I kidding, this is way too complicated a concept, I'm rambling, she has no idea what I'm saying,* so I let it go. When she was done practicing, I went to go get dressed. In my closet I have a word-of-the-day calendar, and I saw that it was still on yesterday's date. I tore off the page. Today's word: *acoustics.*

See also: Meaning

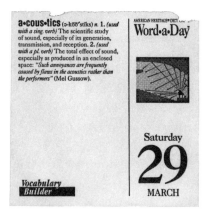

American Heritage Dictionary Word-a-Day Calendar, 2003.

Wordplays

I am bewitched by the perfection of the American Youth Soccer Organization (AYSO)'s bumper sticker: PLAYSOCCER.

Similarly, when Paul Newman ventured out into the cookie market with his Fig Newmans, I thought, *Well, regardless of how they taste, I must support this new product because the name is genius.* I could see them brainstorming, sitting around a conference table with a huge pad of paper and a thick black marker, and everyone throwing out salad dressing ideas. *How about Tarragon and Honey Mustard? How about Soy Miso?* And one guy goes, *Hey, wouldn't it be funny to do a cookie called Fig Newmans?* And everyone laughs, ha-ha, *Clever name, but we make salad dressing, not cookies, let's move on, next idea.* And then this guy, who is beside himself over having come up with such a brilliant name, decides to write a memo to Mr. Paul Newman himself, what the hell, and he works on a draft of this letter for days, finally sends it off (after agonizing over which stamp at the post office: flag design or Emily Brontë; went with the flag), and then three days later—just three days!—he gets an e-mail from Paul himself. He and Joanne love the idea. (Joanne!) I like to think this is how Fig Newmans were born.

See also: Amy Rosenthal; E; Encyclopedia Spine; Sign at 7-Eleven

WORDS THAT LOOK SIMILAR

| applause | EXIT | bestseller | utterly |
| applesauce | EXCITE | be stellar | butterfly |

WOW

The word *WOW* hangs on the back wall of my studio office. I bought the three jumbo letters years ago, at an antique shop; they were salvaged from an old Woolworth's sign. When I picture my studio, I picture that big red exclamation.

Shortly after September 11, Jason spent the afternoon painting in the studio. When he emerged at suppertime, I asked if I could go see. I took one step into the studio and was blown away. The painting was magnificent—colorful, throbbing, alive, shattering. I pointed to the number stenciled in black down the side. *The ZIP code of the World Trade Center,* he said. Yes, of course.

I stood back a bit to take it all in. Something looked different . . . What's diff— Oh, okay, I see, there's a letter missing from my back wall. There it is, on the floor. He took down the first *W* while he was painting to make room for his oversized canvas. I *knew* something was different. And wait a second, that's eerie—the wall has had a change of heart; it, too, has sobered up. It's now saying the same thing the painting is: OW.

Wreck

I have this strange sensation when I turn on a light and the bulb—fizzle, spark—goes out. My split-second reaction is, *Wait, no, I just turned the light on wrong, let me do it again, I'm sure the light will work.* I want a do-over. Of course, I know this is nonsense. The light is out. And that is that. I'm just saying.

A couple summers ago, we journeyed to Greece. One afternoon we took an island boat ride to a tiny patch of beach surrounded by huge jagged cliffs. The main attraction, however, wasn't the landscape itself, but a shipwreck, a large, old rusty boat plopped sideways on the sand.

A picture of that shipwreck hung in my sparse European bedroom, so I had looked at this photo for days. There are no people in the photo, just the beach and the ship. So I was shocked to find, as our tourist boat dropped anchor at the shore, hordes of visitors climbing aboard and running around the ship. We didn't go over to the shipwreck right away; we stood there and tried to consciously suck in the beauty and the remoteness. We felt, despite our extreme southern latitude, on top of the world.

The kids were eager to explore the wreck. From the first rickety crooked ladder, I realized that this ship was not the world's safest toy. There were tons of kids running around the ship, but this didn't comfort me as much as I wished it would. My heartbeat increased with each creak. Jason was down below on the sand, watching us through the lens of his spiffy new digital camera. All I could think about was rounding up the kids and getting the hell off the boat.

We soon found ourselves on one of the ship's gangways. This particular stretch had a few planks missing. Looking down through the hole, I saw sand where the bottom of the ship would have been, about fifteen feet below. The gap was no more than one foot wide, so the kids could easily jump across it; for me it was just a big step. Justin went first and jumped. I waited for Miles to go—he was right in front of me, his shirtless back against my tummy. Suddenly he spotted a little Greek girl he had played with at the local taverna a couple nights before. I was saying *yes, sweetie, I see her, yes* as he was simultaneously pointing ahead and turning around to make sure I heard him. I remember feeling rather impatient because I just wanted to get on with it, to cross over this hole. *Yes, I see the girl, now on with it.* And with that, Miles was gone. He slipped right through.

To be honest, my first emotion was sort of annoyance-disbelief-anger, like the *what are you doing?!* reaction you might have upon discovering your toddler has emptied the entire bottle of shampoo into the tub. I couldn't believe he had just let himself fall through the crack. *Why did you do that? I'm so mad at you for doing that!* That was the first millisecond. The second millisecond was, *Oh my God, he has just fallen from the top of the ship to the bottom.* I screamed his name. He was screaming mine, Mommy Mommy Mommy! I'm coming, Miles, I'm coming.

I scooped up his light little body and held him, scared to even look at what physical harm had come to him. There was lots of blood, but I sensed instinctively that he wasn't seriously injured. Jason arrived. We ran to the home base—our boat—and they directed us to the captain. By now I could see he had a gouge the entire length of his forearm, but it was just one cut. We counted our blessings. One, two, three, a million.

Days later Miles and I were still talking about the event. We'd look at each other and know what the other was thinking. *I'm thinking about it. Me, too.* In fact, I couldn't stop looking at him. I was enamored with him. *My Miles, you're here. Look at you. I'm so happy you're here. We got so very, very lucky. You're here.*

I saw my child slip away from me. That's what he did. He literally just—there one minute, not there the next—slipped away. I saw, with front-row-seat clarity, just how quickly, randomly, and mercilessly your child can be taken away.

Back in the days when children were allowed to sit in the front seat, I used to tease my mom that throwing her arm out in front of me when she had to abruptly stop the car wouldn't do squat. Nonetheless, there would go her arm, landing an inch from my face at about chin level. Of course, now I understand; in fact, that's pretty much how I'd like to escort my kids through the world, with my arm extended, shielding them, lifting it only when I am sure the coast is clear.

Miles slipped away. Then he came back. But now I know, in the saddest, most awful place my heart can imagine, that sometimes when the light goes out, it's just out.

WRITING TOOLS

How much of a writer's style (and success?) is influenced or even determined, helped or hindered, by the standard writing tool of his time? For example, how would typing on a computer have changed Shakespeare's body of work? Was it simply his destiny to arrive at *to be or not to be, that is the question* regardless of whether he wrote by hand, typewriter, or computer, or would there be distinct versions, different shades of that phrase, depending on which machine the initial thought had been grinded through? Perhaps Socrates cut short a particular exploration because he couldn't muster up the energy to rewrite it for the twenty-ninth time. What if Proust had access to Microsoft Word—would entire passages of *Remembrance of Things Past* have fallen victim to the ravenous delete button? Would the book's structure be entirely something different because of the ease of cutting and pasting? Mark Twain relied on dictation. He found writing by hand to be an impediment to his work, sidetracking him into pointless reflection. *The gait and style and movement are not suited to narrative,* he said. What if, instead of on a laptop, I wrote this book with ink and feather?

X

X, Marking with

Please *X* accordingly.

	Never	Sometimes	Often	Always
I wash new clothes before I wear them	——	——	——	——
I feel content most of the time.	——	——	——	——
I return books that I borrow from friends.	——	——	——	——
I break out in a rash after eating shellfish.	——	——	——	——
I like myself.	——	——	——	——
I notice different kinds of chairs.	——	——	——	——
I tell the truth even if it means hurting someone's feelings.	——	——	——	——
I keep fresh fruit out in a large wooden bowl.	——	——	——	——
I worry about being buried alive.	——	——	——	——

	Never	Sometimes	Often	Always
I can be genuinely happy for someone else's success regardless of my own personal success/failure status at the moment.	—	—	—	—
I go out of my way to help tourists.	—	—	—	—
I wonder if I am going about it all wrong.	—	—	—	—
I brush my tongue.	—	—	—	—
I think of myself as a citizen of the world.	—	—	—	—
I say yes when the server asks me if I would like pepper on my salad.	—	—	—	—
I come to another's defense if I feel they are being treated or spoken about unfairly.	—	—	—	—
I iron my jeans.	—	—	—	—
I have been unfaithful.	—	—	—	—
I believe in God.	—	—	—	—
I believe in magic.	—	—	—	—

XX

I like being a girl. I like the clothes that go with the gender: tank tops, jeans, short patterned skirts, flared pants. I would not like to have to wear a suit every day; I think I would find it boring, not to mention the choking constriction of the tie and top buttoned dress shirt. And the shoes are better, too, I think. I like that as a girl I basically never have to feel obligated to play rough—football especially, that really does not appeal to me. I feel that I am on the bonus end of some sexist habits: for example, in the winter I get to wait in the restaurant's warm entryway while my husband goes and pulls the car around. Perhaps I should offer to reciprocate, but this never seems to be even mildly expected. The door thing, I can go either way on that; I like when it is held for me, but also like the feeling of doing my part when I hold it for others, be it male, female, or child. I suppose we girls do get the short end of the stick when it comes to taking our tops off in the hot weather: I always envied boys that, and think how freeing and pleasant it must feel, particularly the first moment, the contrast between sticky sweaty T-shirt and slight breeze on exposed skin. Even with the legendary long restroom lines, I would still say female trumps male based on the private stalls versus urinals alone. Even the word itself is awful: *urinal.* As mere letters on paper it still manages to release a certain stench and make one grimace. I have to say I never much minded the whistling or *hey baby*-ing, maybe because it doesn't happen all that often to me, and also because early on I discovered a leveling response that feels comfortable (tossing a quick peace sign their way) and that simultaneously acknowledges the fellow and shuts him up. I'd say, if you are going to be a girl, all in all, now is a pretty good time: we can choose, vote, walk down the street without a veil, escort or curfew, hunt, gather or both.

Y

You

Perhaps you think I didn't matter because I lived _____ years ago, and back then life wasn't as lifelike as it is to you now; that I didn't truly, fully, with all my senses, experience life as you are presently experiencing it, or think about _____ as you do, with such intensity and frequency.

But I was here.

And I did things.

I shopped for groceries. I stubbed my toe. I danced at a party in college and my dress spun around. I hugged my mother and father and hoped they would never die. I pulled change from my pocket. I wrote my name with my finger on a cold, fogged-up window. I used a dictionary. I had babies. I smelled someone barbecuing down the street. I cried to exhaustion. I got the hiccups. I grew breasts. I counted the tiles in my shower. I hoped something would happen. I had my blood pressure taken. I wrapped my leg around my husband's leg in bed. I was rude when I shouldn't have been. I watched the celloist's bow go up and down, and adored the music he made. I picked at a scab. I wished I was older. I wished I was younger. I loved my children. I loved mayonnaise. I sucked my thumb. I chewed on a blade of grass.

I was here, you see. I was.

[The end.]

Permissions

"Busy" entry originally appeared in *The New York Times* (June 3, 1999).

"Wreck" entry will appear in *Parenting Magazine,* March 2005.

Grateful acknowledgment is made to the following for permission to reprint
previously published and unpublished material:
Bruce Bendinger:
"Flahoolick" from *The Book of Gossage,* by Howard Gossage and Bruce Bendinger.
Reprinted by permission of the author.
Houghton Mifflin Company:
"March 29th, 2003" from *The American Heritage Dictionary Word-a-Day Calendar*
from *The American Heritage Dictionary of the English Language, Fourth Edition.*
Dictionary entry and art copyright © 2000 by Houghton Mifflin Company.
Reprinted by permission of Houghton Mifflin Company.
Permission for calendar format given by Andrews McMeel Publishing.
All rights reserved.
The Kenneth Koch Literary Estate:
"You Want a Social Life, with Friends" from "Songs from the Plays"
found in *Straits* by Kenneth Koch (Alfred A. Knopf, New York, 1998).
Reprinted by permission of The Kenneth Koch Literary Estate.
Tony Rogers:
Excerpts from "Tony's Dream" by Tony Rogers.
Reprinted by permission of the dreamer.
Jon Spayde:
Excerpt from piece on "Wabi-Sabi," originally appeared in *Utne Reader*
(August 8, 2001). Reprinted by permission of the author.

Grateful acknowledgment is made to the following for permission to reprint
illustrative material:
Encyclopaedia Britannica, Inc.:
Image of spine of a volume of *Encyclopaedia Britannica* (page 96) courtesy
of Encyclopaedia Britannica, Inc. Reprinted with permission.
Charise Mericle Harper:
"Thursday" painting (page 77) courtesy of Charise Mericle Harper.
Reprinted by permission of the artist.
Lois Gibson:
Forensic sketches of Amy Krouse Rosenthal (page 118) rendered by Lois Gibson
(LoisGibson.com), pastel on Canson Mi Tientes paper approximately 12" × 9".
Reprinted by permission of the artist.
John Scott:
Yoga positions chart (page 3) courtesy of John Scott.
Reprinted by permission of the artist.

ABOUT THE AUTHOR

Amy Krouse Rosenthal is, alphabetically, an author of
adult and children's books; contributor to magazines
and NPR; host of the literary and music variety show
Writers' Block Party on Chicago Public Radio; and mother
of some kids. She lives in Chicago.

Visit www.encyclopediaofanordinarylife.com.